Introduction

*W*elcome to New Readers Press's *Voyager 8*. In this book, you will build your reading, writing, listening, and speaking skills. You will work with familiar types of reading selections, such as essays, stories, articles, poems, biographies, and excerpts from novels and plays. You will also work with charts and graphs.

This book has four units. Each unit is based on a theme that reflects our day-to-day lives. In *Voyager 8,* you will explore these themes:

- ▶ The Working Experience
- ▶ Breaking New Ground
- ▶ Resolving Conflict
- ▶ Attitudes toward Work

Within each theme-based unit, you will find three lessons. Each lesson has the following features:

- ▶ **Before You Read:** information and an activity to help you prepare for the reading selection, including instructions on previewing the selection and a strategy to use while reading it
- ▶ **Reading:** an essay, poem, article, biographical sketch, excerpt from a novel or play, or other type of reading
- ▶ **Revisit Your Strategy:** an activity that helps you judge whether you used a reading strategy effectively
- ▶ **After You Read:** questions and activities about the reading
- ▶ **Think About It:** practice with a skill that will help you understand, apply, or analyze what you read
- ▶ **Write About It:** an activity to improve your writing skills

In the back of this book, you will find an Answer Key that contains answers for the activities in Revisit Your Strategy, After You Read, and Think About It, plus the Writing Skills Mini-Lessons and the Unit Reviews. Following that is a Reference Handbook, which contains information from the Writing Skills Mini-Lesson in each unit and an outline of the writing process.

We hope you enjoy exploring the themes and mastering the skills found in *Voyager 8*.

Skills Preview

This preview will give you an idea of the kinds of readings and skills covered in this book. Before you begin Unit 1, please complete the entire preview. Then share your work with your instructor.

Reading Skills Preview

Read each selection and answer the questions that follow.

Two Worlds

Jim Yoshida, with Bill Hosokawa

When I was fifteen years old and a freshman in a Seattle high school, I stood 5 feet 7 inches tall and weighed 168 pounds. Many of my friends signed up to try out for the freshman football team. I couldn't because I had to go to Japanese school.

Still, I figured it wouldn't hurt to watch football practice for a little while. I sat on the sidelines, glancing at my watch frequently to make sure I would leave in time to get to Japanese school. On the third day of practice, the freshmen engaged in a scrimmage, and I couldn't tear myself away. I had played some sandlot football, and I figured I could do just as well as the freshmen in uniform. Before I knew it, it was too late to get to Japanese school on time. It didn't take me long to rationalize that being absent was only a little worse than being tardy. I decided that I might just as well watch football practice for the remainder of the day. Before long, nothing seemed to be more important than playing football with the freshman team. I approached the coach and told him I wanted to try out.

Coach Heaman looked at my stocky frame. "What's your name?" he asked.

"Jim Yoshida," I replied.

He reached into a pocket and pulled out a form. "You have to get your parents' permission," he said. "Take this home and get it signed. Come down to the locker room after school tomorrow and check out a uniform."

My heart sank. Here I was being invited to try out for the team, and parental permission—an impossible obstacle—blocked the way.

Full of apprehension, I went home at the normal time. Apparently Mom was unaware of my absence from Japanese school, and if my sister Betty had noticed, she hadn't said anything. I knew that Mom could sense when I had something on my mind. Besides, I wanted to talk to her before Dad came home, so I came straight to the point.

"Mom," I ventured, "I want to try out for the football team at school."

After hesitating a moment she replied, "What if you were injured playing football? Besides, what would you do about Japanese school? I think you had better forget about football."

I knew it was useless to try to change her mind and even more useless to talk to Dad.

Next day during a study period, I gave myself permission to play football. My hands were clammy when I gave the slip to Coach Heaman. I was sure he could hear the pounding of my heart and see the look of guilt that I knew was written on my face. He failed to notice, however, and routinely filed the permission form and issued me an ancient, hand-me-down uniform and a pair of ill-fitting shoes.

I made the team as a running guard. This meant I pulled out of the line and ran interference for the ballcarrier. If I did what I was supposed to do and threw a good block, the ballcarrier had a chance of making a good gain.

At the end of the freshman season, I was one of several freshman players invited to suit up with the varsity. In the season finale, the varsity coach let me play half the game.

Meanwhile, for some reason I have never understood, my absence from Japanese school went unnoticed until Betty brought home her Japanese-school report card right after the football season ended. Mom and Dad grinned as they examined her record. I knew what was coming next; Dad turned to me and asked to see my report card.

"Sir," I said, "I don't have one."

His eyebrows shot up. "Why not? Did you lose it?"

"No, sir. I haven't been attending Japanese school."

He fixed me with a stare that bored right through me. We were at the dinner table, and all of us had hot boiled rice to eat with cooked meat and vegetables. Steam rose from the bowl in front of my father, and I could see his temper rising too.

"Explain yourself," Dad ordered.

So I told him the whole story, including the way I had signed the form, and his frown grew darker and darker. Mom averted a very explosive situation by suggesting that the dinner table was not the place for a scolding. She suggested we finish our dinner and then talk about the problem.

Sometime during the meal, Dad must have seen the humor of my transgression. Perhaps he remembered pranks he had pulled as a boy. I was relieved to see his anger had given way to simply a serious mood when finally the dishes were cleared away.

First he lectured me about how wrong it was to deceive one's parents, and I had to agree with him. Eventually he got around to football. "I can understand why you would want to play the game," he said. "You should, however, take an interest in a Japanese sport like judo."

Judo is like wrestling, a sport in which a smaller and weaker person learns to use an opponent's strength to defeat the opponent. I didn't have much enthusiasm for judo.

Dad was saying, "Judo will give you the discipline you need. You must learn to grow tougher physically, mentally, and morally."

Then I saw a way that I might be able to play football next season. I apologized for what I had done. I *was* truly sorry. I agreed to go back to Japanese school and try my best to make up for what I had missed. I said I would go to judo class—if I could play football again next year.

The smile that had started to take shape on Dad's face vanished. Then he said, "All right, play football if it's that important to you, but remember there are things that are important to me too. So go to Japanese school and try to learn a little about the language; and go to judo classes and learn a little about discipline." We shook hands.

Several nights later, when I came home from Japanese school, Dad introduced me to a man who was about ten years older than I. His name was Kenny Kuniyuki; he was an instructor at a judo school. Dad told me Kenny would be my judo teacher. I liked Kenny immediately. We had dinner together, and then he drove me to the judo school.

For the next three weeks, every Monday, Wednesday, and Friday, I went to the school and learned to fall. Falling without hurting yourself is an art in itself. Gradually I learned to roll to absorb the impact as I hit the mat and to break the momentum with my arms and legs and shoulders before I crashed to the floor. Then Kenny began on the holds and throws. From seven to nine-thirty I would practice throwing and being thrown with the other students. After everyone else had left, Kenny had me stay and practice with him.

I must admit that I thought about quitting, especially on mornings after a particularly strenuous workout. I knew, though, that if I dropped judo, I could forget about playing football.

Approximately six months after I began judo lessons, everything began to fall into place. I was tough physically; I had learned, finally, to take the hardest falls without hurting myself; and I was able to coordinate my skill with my strength. I found a new exhilaration and excitement in judo. Judo was as much fun as football!

Soon I was good enough to skip over all the intermediate steps—yellow, green, brown, and purple—and get a black belt. It usually takes a student three or four years of hard work to win black-belt rating. I had done it in a fraction of that time. Mom and Dad beamed approval.

Dad raised no objection when I turned out for football in the fall of my sophomore year. I had kept my end of the bargain, and he kept his. I made the team as a running guard and was lucky enough to be an all-city selection even though we didn't win a single game. I still continued practicing my judo after the daily football workouts.

When I returned to school for my junior year, I had 190 muscular pounds on my 5-foot-9½-inch frame. The judo training had given me a better sense of balance, which helped me as a football player. I had no trouble making the team, and at the end of the season, I was again named all-city.

By the time my senior year rolled around, both my parents had become ardent football fans, and they came to watch me play. My new coach shifted me to fullback. I guess the move was a success because even though we still didn't win a game, we scored a touchdown—the first in three years. I was the one who carried the ball over the line! As I picked myself up after scoring, I saw Dad standing just outside the end zone with a big grin on his face. I think the sight of that grin made me the happiest of all!

1. What was Jim Yoshida's main problem?
   (1) He wanted to play football but knew his parents would object.
   (2) He was likely to get injured playing football.
   (3) His parents took little interest in him.
   (4) He did not like going to Japanese school.

2. What solution did Jim and his father develop?
   (1) If Jim learned to play football and took judo lessons, he could drop out of Japanese school.
   (2) If Jim went to Japanese school and learned judo, he could continue to play football.
   (3) If Jim went to Japanese school and played football, he wouldn't have to learn judo.
   (4) If Jim succeeded at Japanese school, he could learn judo and play football.

3. Jim started taking judo soon after
   (1) his freshman year
   (2) the freshman football season
   (3) his sophomore year
   (4) his Japanese school graduation

4. Why do you think Jim's parents wanted him and his sister to go to Japanese school?
   (1) They did not like the American culture.
   (2) They felt their children had too much free time after school.
   (3) They saw it as punishment for disobeying them.
   (4) They wanted their children to learn about the culture of their ancestors.

A Broken Water Hose

Andrew A. Rooney

People who really know how to do something and have the ambition to do it are hard to find.

Several weeks ago I was driving the old station wagon home on a hot summer Sunday night. I started to smell something burning. You know how that is. You hope it's the car next to you or something from the outside air. Finally I couldn't deny that it emanated from under my very own hood. I pulled off the highway into a combination gas station, grocery store and garage. It wasn't the kind of place that gives you any confidence that they know much about cars. I judged my chance of getting anything done there at seven o'clock Sunday evening to be near zero but it was the only choice I had.

Not wishing to irritate the attendant by making him come out to ask what I wanted, I shut off my steaming engine, hurried out of the car and went inside. A paunchy, balding man in his middle forties was closing the cash register on the change he had just collected from the sale of a bag of potato chips.

"Yeah?" he said in a tone that suggested he didn't have time for me.

I told him my problem. He came out to the car and as I unlatched the hood, he lifted it and was instantly engulfed in a cloud of steam.

When the fog cleared he just shook his head.

"I dunno," he said. "You got a broken water hose here."

He went back into the store, sold two Hostess Twinkies and then went into the one-pit garage connected to the store.

I waited, uncertain about whether he'd abandoned me or not. Pretty soon he emerged with a length of hose. I was tense. He tried to fit the piece of hose on the pipe leading from the radiator but it wasn't close to the right size.

"May not have it," he said.

I was fifty miles from home. I had about twenty-seven dollars on me and didn't know anyone nearby I could call.

The man disappeared into the garage again and this time I was sure he'd lost interest in my case. When he finally emerged he had two more pieces of hose. Neither of them fitted but I knew by now that I had someone special here. This fellow had taken on my problem for his own and he was sticking at it. It was a dirty little job but he was helping me.

For the next forty-five minutes he'd wrestle with a piece of hose under my hood for a while and then go in and sell something or pump fifteen gallons of gas, but he always came back to me.

I had been there perhaps an hour when he finally found a length of hose that fit. I was happy, relieved and grateful. I could hardly believe this fellow had kept at the job until he got it done.

Next, of course, I was worried about my twenty-seven dollars. I would have been happy to pay him one hundred and twenty-seven dollars if I'd had it, but I didn't, and there was no way of knowing what he'd charge.

He went into the store area as I followed along like a faithful dog, grateful for anything my master was doing for me. Inside he took a greasy parts book down off the shelf behind him. When they go for the parts book, I'm nervous.

His finger went up and down several pages, as he uttered an occasional grunt. I don't want to suggest this fellow was a lot of fun, but by now I liked him and hoped I'd be able to pay him what he asked. Finally his finger came to rest on a serial number with a price after it.

"2749-16 JDT," he said. "I'll just charge on the cost of the hose. That'll be ten dollars and eighty-five cents."

I have no aberrant tendencies but I could have kissed this man.

"Listen," I said. "It's worth more than that to me. I've only got twenty-seven dollars. Please take the twenty dollars. I'll keep the seven dollars to get to work on in the morning."

Since that episode, I've thought of him a hundred times. Does he make as good a living as he would if he'd told me to get lost, as so many would have under similar circumstances? I hope so. I hope he gets his reward in satisfaction but I hope it turns out that it's also a good way to run a business.

Not many people are running them that way.

5. Which statement below is an example of subjective writing?
   (1) "I hope he gets his reward in satisfaction."
   (2) "I was driving the old station wagon home on a hot summer Sunday night."
   (3) "I had about twenty-seven dollars on me and didn't know anyone nearby I could call."
   (4) "I had been there perhaps an hour when he finally found a length of hose that fit."

6. The second paragraph describes the narrator's increasing feeling of
   (1) confidence
   (2) denial
   (3) hope
   (4) dread

Short Biography of a Washerwoman

Yolanda Ulloa

Emilia
strung the lines of white laundry
toward the horizon
and the suds grew
leaving no trace between her hands

Emilia's back
curved
like a flower
in the heat of the day.
She passed, unhurried, between the laundry
then faded away.

7. The author compares Emilia's back to a flower that has curved in the heat of the day. The author is suggesting that Emilia
   (1) is warm and sweet-smelling
   (2) needs to take a break and get some water
   (3) is tired and weakened from her work
   (4) should improve her posture

8. Emilia is a worker who
   (1) disappears when no one is watching
   (2) loves the feel of soapsuds between her fingers
   (3) needs to pick up her pace to get the work done
   (4) quietly and steadily does her job

Supportive Services
Needed to Attend Training

This graph shows the types of support services that 407 residents in one public housing facility in Chicago say they need to attend job training.

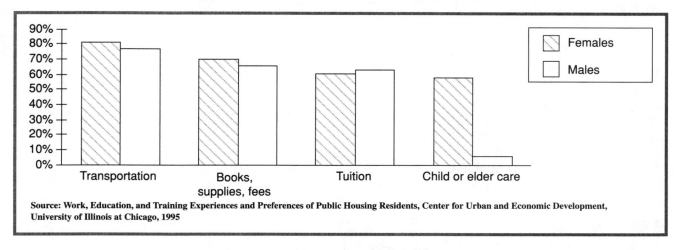

Source: Work, Education, and Training Experiences and Preferences of Public Housing Residents, Center for Urban and Economic Development, University of Illinois at Chicago, 1995

9. One difference between the men and the women in this group that you can infer from the graph is that
   (1) the men pay more for tuition than the women do
   (2) the women take more responsibility for child and elder care
   (3) more of the men than the women can drive
   (4) the women buy more books and supplies than the men do

10. The information in the graph would be most useful to local officials who are
    (1) developing a transportation program across town
    (2) approving college scholarships for people with low incomes across the country
    (3) trying to improve attendance at job training programs that serve this Chicago housing project
    (4) building day-care centers in inner-city Philadelphia

Write About It

On a separate piece of paper, write about the topic below. Then use the Revising Checklist to revise your draft.

Topic: What experiences in your life have had a big effect on you? Think about an experience that changed you by teaching you something about life. Write about this personal experience.

Revising Checklist

Revise your draft. Check that your draft
_____ states the lesson that you learned or the change that took place
_____ states the events that happened to you in the order in which they happened
_____ includes details about the experience
_____ includes your personal thoughts and feelings about the experience

Skills Preview Answers

Reading Skills Preview

1. (1)
2. (2)
3. (2)
4. (4)
5. (1)
6. (4)
7. (3)
8. (4)
9. (2)
10. (3)

Write About It

Make any changes on your first draft that will improve your writing. Then recopy your draft and share it with your instructor.

Skills Chart

The questions in the Skills Preview assess familiarity with the following skills:

Question	Skill
1	analyze problems and solutions
2	analyze problems and solutions
3	understand chronological order
4	make inferences
5	recognize objective/subjective writing
6	identify mood
7	analyze writer's craft, compare
8	understand characterization
9	make inferences, contrast
10	apply information

Unit 1 The Working Experience

What is "the working experience"? It is all that you think, see, feel, hear, and do when you are at work. Whether you sell shoes, work in a factory, tend a garden, manage a business, drive a taxi, or have some other type of job, you work at specific tasks, make decisions, learn and use skills.

Each person's working experience, however, is also different. In this unit, you will learn about the life of a hardworking farm wife. You will read about the experiences of factory workers. And you will analyze several graphs to see how the working experience has changed for Americans over the past 100 years.

Before you begin Unit 1, think about a job you have had or a job you want. What kinds of work experiences have you had? What kind would you like to have?

▶ **Be an Active Reader**

As you read the selections in this unit
- Put a question mark (?) by things you do not understand.
- Underline words you do not know. Try to use context clues to figure them out.

After you read each selection in this unit
- Reread sections you marked with a question mark. If they still do not make sense, discuss them with a partner or your instructor.
- Look at words you underlined. Discuss any words you still don't understand with a partner or your instructor, or look them up in a dictionary.

Lesson 1

Strategy: Empathize as you read
Reading: Read a personal essay
Skill: Understand a characterization
Writing: Write a character sketch

Before You Read

The author of "My Mother Never Worked" describes her mother's experience raising a family and working on the family farm for 50 years, beginning in 1921.

Before you read this personal essay, think about the work done by a homemaker. Then check whether you believe each statement about homemakers is generally true or false.

T	F	
____	____	**1.** A homemaker does not work as hard as a full-time worker in business.
____	____	**2.** A homemaker is not paid for work or for holidays and vacation time.
____	____	**3.** Unpaid homemakers work fewer hours than paid workers.
____	____	**4.** A homemaker needs to learn skills for the job just like any other worker.
____	____	**5.** A person who works as a homemaker for 50 years will receive the same government benefits as someone who works in industry for 50 years.
____	____	**6.** Instead of working when the children go to school, most homemakers watch talk shows and soap operas on television.

Preview the Reading

Preview "My Mother Never Worked" to get some idea of what you are about to read. From the title and the author's name, you will see that a woman is writing about her mother. Look also at the lines of dialogue at the beginning of the essay, as well as the illustration. These features will give you more clues about the essay.

Set Your Strategy: Empathize as You Read

To **empathize** means to identify with another person's feelings. You put yourself in another person's shoes to understand how he or she feels. If you can empathize with people you read about, you will better understand what you read. As you read "My Mother Never Worked," try to feel as the people in the essay felt. After you finish, you will have a chance to identify how you think they felt.

One definition of work *is "effort in doing or making something."*
If this is true, are full-time homemakers workers? Does our society
value their work and their contribution?

My Mother Never Worked

Bonnie Smith-Yackel

"Social Security Office." (The voice answering the telephone sounds very self-assured.)

"I'm calling about . . . I . . . my mother just died . . . I was told to call you and see about a . . . death-benefit check, I think they call it. . . ."

"I see. Was your mother on Social Security? How old was she?"

"Yes . . . she was seventy-eight. . . ."

"Do you know her number?"

"No . . . I, ah . . . don't you have a record?"

"Certainly. I'll look it up. Her name?"

"Smith. Martha Smith. Or maybe she used Martha Ruth Smith. . . . Sometimes she used her maiden name . . . Martha Jerabek Smith."

"If you'd care to hold on, I'll check our records—it'll be a few minutes."

"Yes. . . ."

Her love letters—to and from Daddy—were in an old box, tied with ribbons and stiff, rigid-with-age leather thongs: 1918 through 1920; hers written on stationery from the general store she had worked in full-time and managed, single-handed, after her graduation from high school in 1913; and his, at first, on YMCA or Soldiers and Sailors Club stationery dispensed to the fighting men of World War I. He wooed her thoroughly and persistently by mail, and though she reciprocated[1] all his feelings for her, she dreaded marriage. . . .

"It's so hard for me to decide when to have my wedding day—that's all I've thought about these last two days. I have told you dozens of times that I won't be afraid of married life, but when it comes down to setting the date and then picturing myself a married woman with half a dozen or more kids to look after, it just makes me sick. . . . I am weeping right now—I hope that some day I can look back and say how foolish I was to dread it all."

They married in February, 1921, and began farming. Their first baby, a daughter, was born in January, 1922, when my mother was 26 years old. The second baby, a son, was born in March, 1923. They were renting farms; my father, besides working his own fields, also was a hired man for two other farmers. They had no capital initially, and had to gain it slowly, working from dawn until midnight every day. My town-bred mother learned to set hens and raise chickens, feed pigs, milk cows, plant and harvest a garden, and can every fruit and vegetable she could scrounge. She carried water nearly a quarter of a mile from the well to fill her wash boilers in order to do her laundry on a scrub board. She learned to shuck grain, feed threshers, shuck and husk corn, feed corn pickers. In September, 1925, the third baby came, and in June, 1927, the fourth child—both daughters. In 1930, my parents had enough money to buy their own farm, and that March they moved all their livestock and belongings themselves, 55 miles over rutted, muddy roads.

In the summer of 1930 my mother and her two eldest children reclaimed a 40-acre field from Canadian thistles, by chopping them all out with a hoe. In the other fields, when the oats and flax began to head out, the green and blue of the crops were hidden by the bright yellow of wild mustard. My mother walked the fields day after day, pulling each mustard plant. She raised a new flock of baby chicks—500—and she spaded up, planted, hoed, and harvested a half-acre garden.

During the next spring their hogs caught cholera[2] and died. No cash that fall.

During the next year the drought hit. My mother and father trudged from the well to the chickens, the well to the calf pasture, the well to the barn, and from the well to the garden. The sun came out hot and bright, endlessly, day after day. The crops shriveled and died. They harvested half the corn, and ground the other half, stalks and all, and fed it to the cattle as fodder. With the price at four cents a bushel for the harvested crop, they couldn't afford to haul it into town. They burned it in the furnace for fuel that winter.

---

1. **reciprocated** (ri/SIP/ro/kayt/ed) gave or showed in return
2. **cholera** (KAW/le/ruh) an often deadly infectious disease of the stomach and intestines

In 1934, in February, when the dust was still so thick in the Minnesota air that my parents couldn't always see from the house to the barn, their fifth child—a fourth daughter—was born. My father hunted rabbits daily, and my mother stewed them, fried them, canned them, and wished out loud that she could taste hamburger once more. In the fall the shotgun brought prairie chickens, ducks, pheasant, and grouse. My mother plucked each bird, carefully reserving the breast feathers for pillows.

In the winter she sewed night after night, endlessly, begging cast-off clothing from relatives, ripping apart coats, dresses, blouses, and trousers to remake them to fit her four daughters and son. Every morning and every evening she milked cows, fed pigs and calves, cared for chickens, picked eggs, cooked meals, washed dishes, scrubbed floors, and tended and loved her children. In the spring she planted a garden once more, dragging pails of water to nourish and sustain the vegetables for the family. In 1936 she lost a baby in her sixth month.

In 1937 her fifth daughter was born. She was 42 years old. In 1939 a second son, and in 1941 her eighth child—and third son.

But the war had come, and prosperity of a sort. The herd of cattle had grown to 30 head; she still milked morning and evening. Her garden was more than a half acre—the rains had come, and by now the Rural Electricity Administration[3] and indoor plumbing. Still she sewed—dresses and jackets for the children, housedresses and aprons for herself, weekly patching of jeans, overalls, and denim shirts. She still made pillows, using the feathers she had plucked, and quilts every year—intricate patterns as well as patch-work, stitched as well as tied—all necessary bedding for her family. Every scrap of cloth too small to be used in quilts was carefully saved and pains-takingly sewed together in strips to make rugs. She still went out in the fields to help with the haying whenever there was a threat of rain.

In 1959 my mother's last child graduated from high school. A year later the cows were sold. She still raised chickens and ducks, plucked feathers, made pillows, baked her own bread, and every year made a new quilt—now for a married child or for a grandchild. And her garden, that huge, undying symbol of sustenance, was as large and cared for as in all the years before. The canning, and now freezing, continued.

In 1969, on a June afternoon, mother and father started out for town so that she could buy sugar to make rhubarb jam for a daughter who lived in Texas. The car crashed into a ditch. She was paralyzed from the waist down.

In 1970 her husband, my father, died. My mother struggled to regain some competence and dignity and order in her life. At the rehabilitation institute, where they gave her physical therapy and trained her to live usefully in a wheelchair, the therapist told me: "She did fifteen pushups

---

3. Rural Electricity Administration U.S. government agency involved in bringing electricity to farm areas of the country

today—fifteen! She's almost seventy-five years old! I've never known a woman so strong!"

From her wheelchair she canned pickles, baked bread, ironed clothes, wrote dozens of letters weekly to her friends and her "half dozen or more kids," and made three patchwork housecoats and one quilt. She made balls and balls of carpet rags—enough for five rugs. And kept all her love letters.

"I think I've found your mother's records—Martha Ruth Smith; married to Ben F. Smith?"

"Yes, that's right."

"Well, I see that she was getting a widow's pension. . . ."

"Yes, that's right."

"Well, your mother isn't entitled to our $255 death benefit."

"Not entitled! But why?"

The voice on the telephone explains patiently:

"Well, you see—your mother never worked."

▶ Revisit Your Strategy: Empathize as You Read

Read each excerpt from "My Mother Never Worked." Put yourself in the character's shoes. Check *all* the words that describe the character's feelings.

1. ▶ "I have told you dozens of times that I won't be afraid of married life, but when it comes down to setting the date and then picturing myself a married woman with half a dozen or more kids to look after, it just makes me sick."

How did Martha Jerabek feel as she wrote those lines?

_____ uncertain	_____ tense	_____ understanding
_____ compassionate	_____ content	_____ torn

2. ▶ "Well, you see—your mother never worked."

How do you think the daughter felt when she heard that?

_____ uncaring	_____ disbelieving	_____ approving
_____ disheartened	_____ disgusted	_____ angry

After You Read

A. Comprehension Check

1. Martha had a hard time setting a date for her wedding because she
   (1) wanted a big wedding but couldn't afford it
   (2) dreaded the idea of a married life
   (3) loved someone else
   (4) was not sure her fiance truly loved her

2. Martha's family did not get a Social Security death benefit because Martha
   (1) had used the benefit while she was alive
   (2) never held a job that paid into the Social Security system
   (3) had gotten a widow's pension
   (4) was too young when she died

3. The one job never performed by Martha was
   (1) managing a general store
   (2) raising eight children
   (3) planting and harvesting
   (4) selling her handmade quilts and housecoats

4. As the farm became more prosperous, Martha continued to sew, make pillows and quilts, and help with the haying because
   (1) these tasks had become a part of her
   (2) she was afraid of being poor again
   (3) her husband demanded it
   (4) she was saving money for retirement

5. You can tell from the essay, the author
   (1) was ashamed of her mother
   (2) thought her mother never worked
   (3) loved and admired her mother
   (4) thought her mother's life was wasted

6. In the sentence, "At the *rehabilitation* institute, where they gave her physical therapy and trained her," *rehabilitation* means
   (1) providing a place to live
   (2) teaching new crafts
   (3) training for athletics
   (4) restoring to usefulness

B. Read between the Lines

Check each statement below that you think the author would agree with. Look back at the essay for evidence to support each statement you check.

_____ 1. Raising a family and maintaining a household are not work.
_____ 2. Martha Smith's work was just as important as a wage earner's.
_____ 3. Homemakers should get Social Security benefits in their name.
_____ 4. Martha Smith always regretted her decision to marry.
_____ 5. Martha Smith was a remarkable woman.

C. Think beyond the Reading

Discuss these questions with a partner. Answer them in writing on separate paper if you wish.

1. Do you believe that homemakers like Mrs. Smith should receive full Social Security benefits? Explain your thinking.
2. What skills did Martha Smith have to learn to become a homemaker and a farm wife in the 1920s? Have your responses to the statements in Before You Read on page 14 changed after reading the essay?

Think About It: Understand Characterization

The way a writer develops characters and portrays them to readers is called **characterization.** The author of "My Mother Never Worked" uses actions, events, and dialogue to reveal Martha Jerabek Smith's character: her personality, beliefs, and values.

A. Look at Characterization

Notice the details the author provides about Martha Jerabek Smith's character traits in the following excerpt from the essay.

> ▶ Her love letters—to and from Daddy—were in an old box, tied with ribbons and stiff, rigid-with-age leather thongs: 1918 through 1920; hers written on stationery from the general store she had worked in full-time and managed, single-handed, after her graduation from high school in 1913; and his, at first, on YMCA or Soldiers and Sailors Club stationery dispensed to the fighting men of World War I. He wooed her thoroughly and persistently by mail, and though she reciprocated all his feelings for her, she dreaded marriage.

Complete the character web below by filling in details from the excerpt and the character traits they suggest Martha Jerabek had.

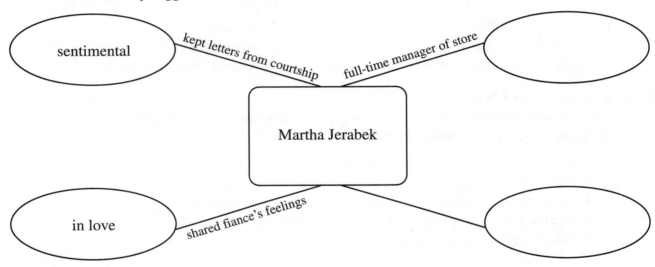

Because Martha was a full-time manager of a general store right after graduation, you probably wrote that she was hardworking, dependable, competent, or able. If you wrote that she dreaded marriage, you could add that she was troubled, worried, or anxious.

 Tip   A writer uses the characters' words, thoughts, and actions for characterization—to provide clues about the characters' personalities, beliefs, and values. Clues are also found in what other characters say and how other characters act toward them.

B. Practice

1. Reread the paragraph on page 16 that starts with "They married in February, 1921 . . ." Then finish the character web that follows.

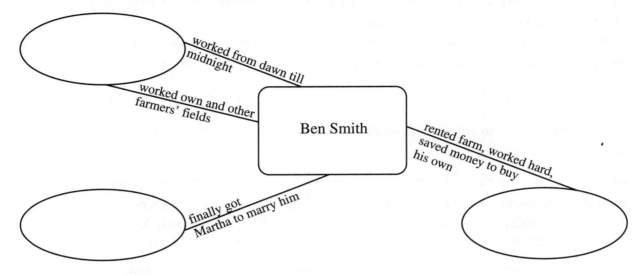

2. Reread the two paragraphs on pages 17–18, starting with "In 1970 her husband, my father, died." and ending with ". . . love letters." Then finish the character web describing Mrs. Smith's character traits after the car accident.

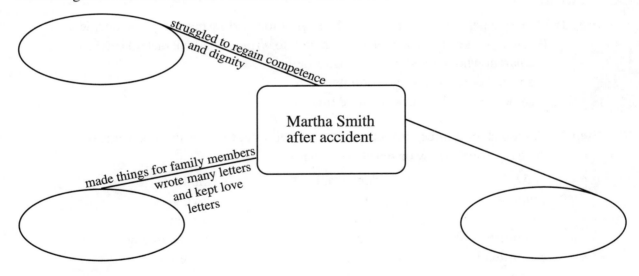

▶ **Talk About It**

You have read about a woman's decision to give up her independence for the hard life of a farm wife, homemaker, and mother. Think of the feelings that would make a daughter write about her mother the way Bonnie Smith-Yackel wrote about Martha Jerabek Smith. Consider the things she chose to include and the way she expressed them. Discuss what these things tell you about the author and her relationship with her mother.

Write About It: Write a Character Sketch

In "My Mother Never Worked," the daughter characterizes her mother as a hardworking, unselfish, and loving woman. Now you will have a chance to write a character sketch about someone you know. A character sketch is an essay in which the writer creates a focused impression of a person by writing about the person's actions, personality, and values. First, study the sample, which shows how to write a character sketch.

Study the Sample

Read the steps below to see what the writer considered as she developed her character sketch.

Step 1: Picking a Topic. The writer of this sample chose to write about her husband.

Step 2: Developing and Organizing Ideas. The writer focused on her husband's relationship with his sister. She chose three character traits—loving, devoted, and gentle. Then she chose examples of his behavior that expressed those traits.

Now read the writer's character sketch on the next page. Then it will be your turn.

Your Turn

A. Prewriting

Step 1: Choose a person to write about. The suggestions below may help you decide. Be sure you know the person well enough to write a good character sketch.
- a parent who worked hard to raise a family
- a friend or co-worker you admire
- someone who has survived hard times

Step 2: Choose at least three character traits that you want to focus on. Use some of the traits listed below or select your own.

brave	dependable	kind
cautious	devoted	loving
clever	energetic	patient
committed	fair	self-confident
controlled	frank	sincere
cooperative	generous	strict
creative	gentle	strong
daring	honest	thoughtful

Step 3: On separate paper, list and organize examples that express the traits you chose. You may want to use a character web to help organize your ideas.

Big Brother

Brian and I awoke to the sounds of pans clanging in the kitchen. "It must be Katie," he said. "I need to check on her." With that, Brian got out of bed, put on his robe, and headed down the stairs to the kitchen.

Katie and Mary had moved in with us the day before. Katie is Brian's sister, and Mary is their mother. Mary, nearly 70, is no longer able to take care of Katie by herself. Katie has Down's syndrome and needs a lot of attention.

I had not been surprised when Brian suggested that the two of them move in with us. Brian is very close to his family, and he and Katie have a special relationship. One of their little rituals began when they were young children. Katie, an early riser, would sit at the kitchen table each morning eagerly awaiting his arrival. Brian would sneak up behind her, give her a big hug, and greet her with "Good morning, Pumpkin!" Katie always laughed with delight and turned to plant a big kiss on his cheek.

Even after Brian and I got married and moved 200 miles away, Brian remained especially devoted to Katie. She came to stay with us for several weeks each summer. Brian would always take two weeks' vacation from his job as a social worker, and we would take trips to Katie's favorite spots—the lake, the amusement park, or the mountains. Katie loved those times—especially when she and Brian went off by themselves.

I decided to stay upstairs and let Brian spend some time alone with Katie. Yesterday she had started to cry uncontrollably. She had been afraid that moving here permanently meant Mary would soon die. Brian, always gentle, comforted her and assured her that this move meant no such thing. He simply wanted Katie and Mary to live with us because he missed them so much.

I listened for what would happen when Brian entered the kitchen. All was quiet for a moment. Then I heard Brian's familiar "Good morning, Pumpkin!" and Katie's delighted laughter filled the house.

B. Writing

On separate paper, write a character sketch about the person you selected.

 Tip When you write your character sketch, use vivid language and details that will make the person come alive for readers.

▶ **Save your draft.** At the end of this unit, you will work with one of your drafts further.

Lesson 2 ▶ LEARNING GOALS

Strategy: Visualize
Reading: Read two poems
Skill: Identify mood
Writing: Write a poem

Before You Read

The poems in this lesson describe the daily routines of night-shift workers and factory workers. Before you read the poems, think about factory work, and especially what it is like to work the night shift in a factory. Then list three words or phrases that come to mind for each of the following.

1. Factory work: _____

_____

2. Nighttime in a factory: _____

_____

3. Home life of a night-shift worker: _____

_____

4. Social life of a night-shift worker: _____

_____

Preview the Reading

Preview the poems "Nightshift Workers" and "Factory Work" to get an idea of what you will read. First, look at the titles of the poems for hints about the type of workers you will read about. Then look at the illustration for more clues about "Nightshift Workers." Finally, skim the lines of the poems for words and phrases that catch your attention. Think about how these words and phrases might be connected.

Set Your Strategy: Visualize

To **visualize** means to mentally picture objects or events. As you read the following two poems, watch for details that create pictures in your mind. When you finish reading the poems, you will have a chance to identify words and phrases that helped you form a mental picture of each poem.

If you worked the night shift, your daily routine would be different
from day workers'. When would you sleep? Run errands? Relax? How would
you feel? Read on to discover some of the experiences of night-shift workers.

Nightshift Workers

George Charlton

They have come from a factory
Where fluorescent strips flared all night

And ears grew numb to machinery;
They are going home to working wives,   (4)

To cooling beds at breakfast time,
Undressing fatigue from their skin like clothes;

Later to wake at four and taste teeth
Soft as fur in their mouths.   (8)

They live in a dislocation of hours
Inside-out like socks pulled on in darkness

Waking when the day is over.
They are always at an ebb, unlike others   (12)

Going out to work in the morning
Where sun and moon shine in the sky together.

What is it like to work an assembly line, standing on your feet for hours,
repeating the same task over and over again? The following poem describes
working on an assembly line in a shoe factory.

Factory Work

Deborah Boe

All day I stand here, like this,
over the hot-glue machine,
not too close to the wheel
that brings up the glue,
and I take those metal shanks,[1]   (5)
slide the backs of them in glue
and make them lie down
on the shoe-bottoms, before the sole
goes on. It's simple, but the lasts[2]
weigh, give you big arms.   (10)
If I hit my boyfriend now,
in the supermarket parking lot,
he knows I hit him.

Phyllis, who stands next to me,
had long hair before the glue machine   (15)
got it. My machine ate up my shirt once.
I tried to get it out, the wheel
spinning on me, until someone with a brain
turned it off. It's not bad
here, people leave you alone,   (20)
don't ask you what you're thinking.

It's a good thing, too, because all this morning
I was remembering last night,
when I really thought my grandpa's soul
had moved into the apartment   (25)
the way the eggs fell, and the lamp
broke, like someone was trying
to communicate to me, and he
just dead this week. I wouldn't
blame him. That man in the next aisle   (30)
reminds me of him, a little.

It's late October now, and Eastland
needs to lay some people off.
Last week they ran a contest
to see which shankers shanked fastest.   (35)
I'm not embarrassed to say
I beat them all. It's all
in economy of motion, all the moves
on automatic. I almost
don't need to look at what   (40)
I'm doing. I'm thinking of the way
the leaves turn red when the cold
gets near them. They fall until
you're wading in red leaves up to your knees,
and the air snaps   (45)
in the tree-knuckles, and you begin
to see your breath rise
out of you like your own ghost
each morning you come here.

---

1. shank the narrow part of a shoe, connecting the broad part
of the sole with the heel
2. lasts blocks of wood or metal shaped like feet, on which
shoes and boots are formed

▶ **Revisit Your Strategy: Visualize**

A. 1. Look back at the poem "Nightshift Workers" to find words and phrases that helped you visualize what the poet was describing. What details helped you picture the factory?

_____

2. What details in the poem helped you picture how the night-shift workers look and feel?

_____

_____

3a. Write a few words or phrases of your own to describe the picture of the factory you created in your mind.

_____

_____

b. Write a few words or phrases of your own that describe the picture of the night-shift workers you created in your mind.

_____

_____

B. 1. Look back at the poem "Factory Work" to find words and phrases that helped you visualize. What details helped you picture what the factory job is like?

_____

_____

_____

2. Write several words or phrases that describe the picture of the speaker in the poem that you created in your mind.

_____

_____

_____

After You Read

A. Comprehension Check

1. When do the workers in "Nightshift Workers" go home?
   (1) in the morning   (3) during lunch time
   (2) during break time   (4) in the evening

2. The night-shift workers' lives seem "inside-out" because they
   (1) pull their socks on in the darkness
   (2) have wives who work the night shift, too
   (3) go to work when the sun and moon are in the sky together
   (4) work when most people sleep and sleep when most people work

3. In the line "They are always *at an ebb* unlike others," *at an ebb* means
   (1) filling up   (3) flowing
   (2) going away   (4) returning

4. In "Factory Work," the speaker's job is to
   (1) make glue   (3) shank shoes
   (2) operate a wheel   (4) repair shoes

5. You can tell that the poet of "Nightshift Workers"
   (1) doesn't care about night-shift workers
   (2) thinks night-shift workers are strange
   (3) feels sympathy for night-shift workers
   (4) doesn't know much about working the night shift

6. The speaker in "Factory Work" thought her grandpa's spirit was trying to communicate with her because
   (1) the man in the next aisle looks like him
   (2) eggs fell and a lamp broke in her apartment
   (3) she was about to be laid off
   (4) a ghost arose from her breath this morning

7. Compared to "Nightshift Workers," the speaker in "Factory Work"
   (1) does more dangerous work
   (2) is better at her job
   (3) seems to like her job
   (4) works longer hours

B. Read between the Lines

Check the statements that are likely to be true. Look back at the poems for evidence to support each answer.

_____ 1. Night-shift workers' eyes and ears need to adjust when workers leave the factory.
_____ 2. Night-shift workers feel more rested because they can sleep during the day.
_____ 3. Night-shift workers don't have much time to spend with their spouses who work.
_____ 4. Factory work is repetitious, monotonous, and can be dangerous.
_____ 5. Factory workers require no training.
_____ 6. The speaker in "Factory Work" has ghosts and spirits on her mind because her grandfather died this week.

C. Think beyond the Reading

Discuss these questions with a partner. Answer them in writing on separate paper if you wish.

1. Look back at your responses to Before You Read on page 24. After reading the poems, would you add to or change any of your answers? Explain.
2. After reading "Nightshift Workers" and "Factory Work," would you want to do the kinds of work described in the two poems? Why or why not?

Think About It: Identify Mood

Mood is the overall feeling you get when you read a literary selection. To create an emotional effect in the reader, authors carefully select and describe the characters, setting, objects, details, and images they use. The poets who wrote "Nightshift Workers" and "Factory Work" carefully chose their words and images in order to create a certain feeling, or mood.

A. Look at Mood

Mood is a part of any work that stirs emotions. You can sense a mood when you enjoy a movie, respond to music, or react to a picture. For example, look at the picture below. How does it make you feel? What overall feeling do you get from the setting, people, and other details?

Read the words or phrases below that describe the setting and the people in the picture:

Supervisor angrily reprimanding a worker in front of others; nervous, silent, unhappy workers; steel beams, metal shelves, no chairs, heavy boxes

What feelings do the setting and these details and images create? Write a word or two on the line below to describe the mood.

A mood of _____

All the details work together to create a mood of stress, tension, and anger.

Tip   To help determine a specific mood, use your ability to visualize and to empathize. Picture the people, setting, objects, and other details and think about how they make you feel.

B. Practice

1a. Reread lines 1–3 of "Nightshift Workers" on page 25. Then list words and phrases from the first three lines that help create a mood.

> **People, Setting, Sights, Sounds, Details**
>
> _____
>
> _____

b. What feelings do the words arouse in you? Choose words from the list below to describe the mood or add one or two of your own.

____ tiredness   ____ fear   ____ harshness   _____

____ suspense   ____ dullness   ____ anger   _____

2a. Reread lines 4–14 of "Nightshift Workers" on page 25. Then list words and phrases from these lines that help create a mood.

> **People, Setting, Sights, Sounds, Details**
>
> _____
>
> _____
>
> _____

b. What feelings do the words arouse in you? Choose words from the list below to describe the mood, or add one or two of your own.

____ frustration   ____ loneliness   ____ isolation   _____

____ depression   ____ wildness   ____ contentment   _____

▶ **Talk About It**

The poem "Nightshift Workers" touches on the lifestyle of people who work a night shift. What questions about the night-shift workers' lives do you have? With a partner, list at least five questions about night-shift workers that you would like to ask. If possible, interview someone who works a night shift. Ask the questions you have listed. Then report your findings to the class.

3a. Reread the first two stanzas of "Factory Work," lines 1–21, on page 26. Then list words and phrases from them that help create a mood.

People, Setting, Sights, Sounds, Details

_____

_____

_____

---

b. What overall mood do the words create? Choose from these words or add your own.

____ competence   ____ lurking danger   ____ heaviness   _____

____ strength   ____ resentment   ____ touches of humor   _____

4a. Reread the last two stanzas of "Factory Work," lines 22–49, on page 26. Then list words and phrases from them that help create a mood.

People, Setting, Sights, Sounds, Details

_____

_____

_____

---

b. What overall mood do the words create? Choose from these words or add your own.

____ confidence   ____ acceptance   ____ positive attitude   _____

____ frustration   ____ sadness   ____ negative attitude   _____

▶ **Talk About It**

Many poems can be interpreted in more than one way. Some people reading "Factory Work" might feel that the overall mood is negative, focusing on the recent death of the poet's grandfather and the facts that winter is coming and that people will be laid off. Others would insist that it is basically positive, pointing out the touches of humor and the facts that the poet is good at her job and seems to be looking forward to autumn. With a small group, discuss the elements in the poem that you base your opinion on.

Write About It: Write a Poem

The authors of "Nightshift Workers" and "Factory Work" describe the work and lifestyle of factory workers. In this section, you will have a chance to write a poem about your own work experience. First, study the sample, which shows how to write a poem.

Study the Sample

Read the steps below to see what the writer considered as he created his own poem.

Step 1: Picking a Topic. The sample poem was written by a young man who once worked cleaning swimming pools. He hated the job. Because it aroused such strong feelings in him, he chose that topic for his poem.

Step 2: Developing and Organizing the Poem. The poet visualized himself as he cleaned a swimming pool. He listed words and phrases that described what he had seen, heard, and felt.

Topic: Pool cleaning—the worst job I ever had

Details: kidney-shaped pool   back-and-forth motion

           blue walls   long hours—hour after hour

           murky water   sunburned

           dense brown goo   tight, aching muscles

           scraping noise   unappreciated

Now read the poem on the next page. Then it will be your turn.

Your Turn

A. Prewriting

Step 1: You can write about one of the topics below or choose a topic of your own.

- a factory job
- an outdoor job
- a job with a large company
- a job with unusual hours
- the best job you ever had
- the worst job you ever had
- the hardest job you ever had
- your dream job

Write your topic here:

_____

Pool Cleaner

I have come to clean it,
Your outsized in-ground pool,
That giant kidney
Walled in blue.
I'll watch the murky water clear
As the dense brown goo
Filters out and slithers up,
Scraping against the sides of the hose.

I am unseen.
Hour after hour,
Gliding the pole back and forth,
Back and forth;
Conscious of my sunburned skin,
The tightness of my aching muscles,
I watch the murky water clear
While you read in the shade at pool's edge
And sip an icy drink.

Step 2: Visualize the people, the setting, and the details related to your topic. Think about the mood you want to create. Now write words and phrases that describe the topic and create the mood.

_____

_____

_____

_____

B. Writing

On separate paper, write a poem about the topic you selected.

Tip   To help you create strong images and an overall mood in your poem, say your descriptive words aloud to yourself and listen for those you want to highlight, repeat, or develop.

 Save your draft. At the end of this unit, you will work with one of your drafts further.

Lesson 3

LEARNING GOALS

Strategy: Summarize a graph
Reading: Read two graphs
Skill: Compare and contrast
Writing: Write a paragraph to compare and contrast

Before You Read

Two graphs in this lesson show statistics about U.S. workers from 1900 to 1994. Think about how the workforce has changed in the last 100 years. What new jobs didn't exist in 1900? Do you know of any jobs that have disappeared?

1. Name two or three occupations that didn't exist 100 years ago.

_____

2. Name two occupations that disappeared or almost disappeared in the 20th century.

_____

3. Think of what you know about reading a graph. Where do you usually see graphs?

_____

4. What kind of information is usually presented in a graph?

_____

Preview the Reading

Graphs present data—factual information usually expressed in numbers, such as statistics or measurements. The data in this lesson is about U.S. workers and their work during the 20th century. Read the title of each graph, the key, and the labels along the bottom (the horizontal axis) and along the side (the vertical axis). These features will give you an idea of what data each graph presents. Notice that one graph is a double bar graph and one is a double line graph.

Set Your Strategy: Summarize a Graph

When you **summarize a graph,** you first identify the basic information the graph presents. Notice if the data shows any general trend. Then write a general statement that tells what the graph is about. Writing a summary statement is a good way to check your understanding of a graph. As you read each graph, think about the basic point each makes and notice how the data supports that point. When you are finished, you will have a chance to select a good summary statement.

During the 20th century, economic developments and new technology have changed the types of occupations in which many Americans work. Some occupations have changed more than others. The graph below shows the percentage of American workers employed in selected occupations in 1900 and 1994. It illustrates some of the changes.

American Workers in Selected Occupations

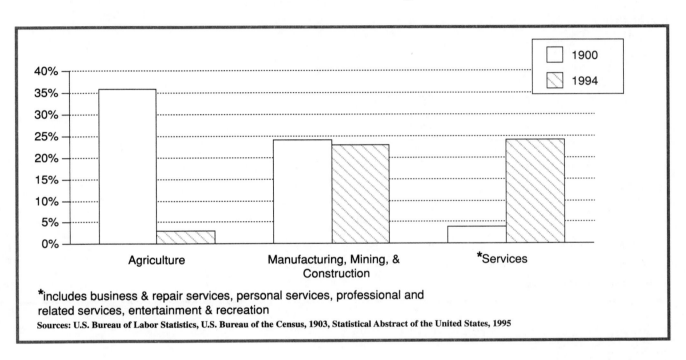

*includes business & repair services, personal services, professional and related services, entertainment & recreation

Sources: U.S. Bureau of Labor Statistics, U.S. Bureau of the Census, 1903, Statistical Abstract of the United States, 1995

▶ **Revisit Your Strategy: Summarize a Graph**

A. Check the statement that best summarizes the graph "American Workers in Selected Occupations."

_____ **1.** In 1900, more than one-third of all American workers worked in agriculture.

_____ **2.** The percentage of people employed in manufacturing, mining, and construction jobs decreased slightly from 1900 to 1994.

_____ **3.** In 1994, about 25 percent of American workers were employed in services.

_____ **4.** In the 20th century, the percentage of American workers in agriculture declined greatly while the percentage in services increased greatly.

Since 1900, the makeup of the U.S. workforce has changed. The graph below shows the percentage of all employable men and women who held nonmilitary jobs in the years given.

Employment Status of Civilian Labor Force*

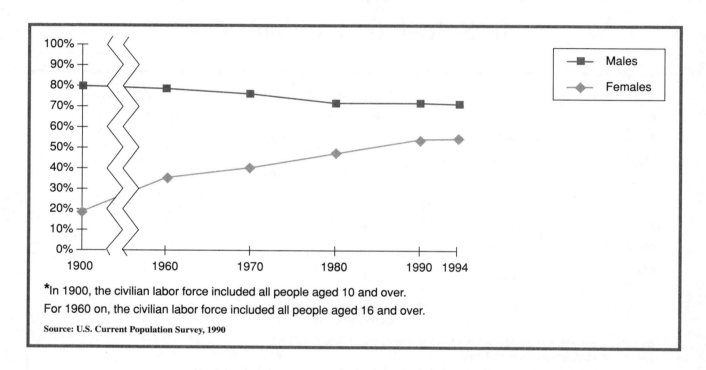

*In 1900, the civilian labor force included all people aged 10 and over.
For 1960 on, the civilian labor force included all people aged 16 and over.

Source: U.S. Current Population Survey, 1990

▶ **Revisit Your Strategy: Summarize a Graph**

B. Check the statement that best summarizes the graph "Employment Status of Civilian Labor Force."

_____ **1.** The percentage of employable women working rose dramatically from 1900 to 1960.

_____ **2.** The percentage of employable men working fell about 10 percent between 1900 and 1994.

_____ **3.** In 1900, most workers were men, but women went to work in steadily increasing percentages throughout the century.

_____ **4.** About 70 percent of men had jobs in 1994; about 55 percent of women did.

After You Read

A. Comprehension Check

1. The graph on page 35 shows that in 1900 about 25 percent of American workers were employed in
   (1) agriculture
   (2) health care
   (3) manufacturing, mining, and construction
   (4) services

2. The graph on page 35 shows that by 1994 the percentage of American workers employed in agriculture had dropped to
   (1) about 35 percent   (3) almost 10 percent
   (2) almost 25 percent   (4) less than 5 percent

3. The graph on page 36 shows that the greatest percentage of women employed in the civilian labor force occurred in
   (1) 1900   (3) 1980
   (2) 1960   (4) 1994

4. The graph on page 36 shows that the greatest percentage of men employed in the civilian labor force occurred in
   (1) 1900   (3) 1980
   (2) 1960   (4) 1994

5. From the graph on page 36, you can tell all of the following *except*
   (1) After 1960, the smallest decrease in percentage of men working happened in the 1980s.
   (2) Fewer men worked in 1994 than in 1900.
   (3) More than half of employable women had civilian jobs by 1990.
   (4) It was uncommon for women to work outside the home in 1900.

B. Read between the Lines

Check the statements that you can reasonably infer from the information in the graphs

According to the graph on page 35
_____ 1. The United States is not the agricultural society it once was.
_____ 2. The demand for services in the United States increased greatly in the 20th century.
_____ 3. There were about the same number of workers in manufacturing, mining, and construction in 1994 as in 1900.

According to the graph on page 36
_____ 4. Women are taking jobs away from men.
_____ 5. By 1960, the federal government had set a minimum age for the civilian labor force.

C. Think beyond the Reading

Discuss these questions with a partner. Answer them in writing on separate paper if you wish.

Why do you think a greater percentage of women worked in 1994 than in 1900? How has the growing percentage of working women affected life in the U.S.? Are there both positive and negative effects? If so, what are they?

Think About It: Compare and Contrast

The graphs on pages 35 and 36 allow you to **compare and contrast** data about the U.S. workforce during the past century. You **compare** the numbers to see how they are similar. You **contrast** the numbers to see how they are different.

A. Look at Compare and Contrast

Read the graph below to compare and contrast the median weekly earnings of full-time male and female workers for selected years from 1983 through 1994. A *median* is the number in the middle. For example, *median weekly earnings of $378* means that the same number of people earned more than $378 as earned less than $378.

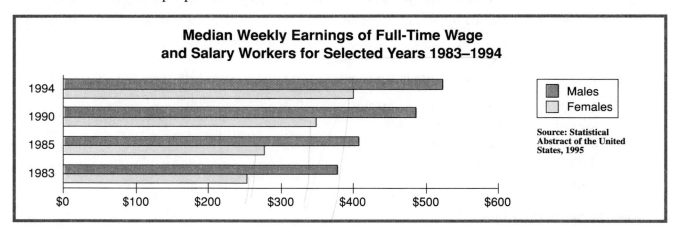

Median Weekly Earnings of Full-Time Wage and Salary Workers for Selected Years 1983–1994

Source: Statistical Abstract of the United States, 1995

Look at the comparison and contrast chart below. How can you tell the information under **Compare** is accurate? How would you fill in the column under **Contrast?**

What does the graph show?	Compare: Look for similarities	Contrast: Look for differences
median weekly earnings of men and women for 1983, 1985, 1990, and 1994	median weekly earnings of both men and women rose between 1983 and 1994	*of both men and women rose between*

You can tell the earnings of both men and women rose by looking at the pairs of bars and seeing both were longer for each later year. By noting how the bar for men is always longer than the bar for women, you can complete the chart by writing under **Contrast,** "Men's median wages were higher than women's in every year shown."

Tip To compare data in graphs, look for ways the numbers are similar. For example, look for bars that are nearly the same length or lines that move in the same way. To contrast data, look for differences, for example, bars of different lengths or lines of different heights.

B. Practice

Read the graph below. Then complete the chart and the summary.

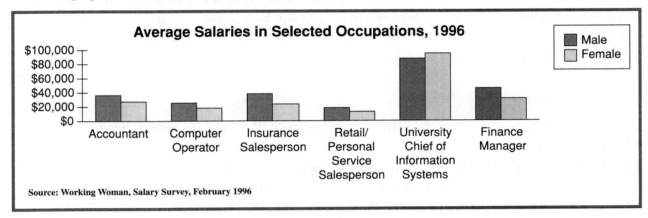

Average Salaries in Selected Occupations, 1996

Legend: ■ Male ☐ Female

Source: Working Woman, Salary Survey, February 1996

1. Compare and contrast information from the graph by completing the chart below.

What does the graph show?	Compare: Look for similarities	Contrast: Look for differences
average salaries of men and women in selected occupations in 1996	most workers shown earned less than $40,000 in 1996	_____ _____
average salaries of financial managers in 1996	_____ _____	average salary of men is significantly higher
average salaries of university information systems chiefs in 1996	highest paid of occupations shown in 1996	_____ _____
average salaries of retail salespersons in 1996	_____ _____	_____ _____

2. In a sentence, summarize the contrast between men's and women's average salaries in 1996 for the occupations shown on the graph.

_____

▶ **Talk About It**

With a partner, use an almanac or other resource to research the average salaries of men and women for four or five other occupations. Compile your results in a bar graph. Then compare and contrast the data in your graph with the graph above. Present your findings to the class.

Write About It: Write a Paragraph to Compare and Contrast

The graphs that you have read in this lesson are similar to the types of graphs you see in reference books, magazines, and newspapers. Now you will have a chance to write a paragraph to compare and contrast information from a graph. First, study the sample, which shows how to write a paragraph to compare and contrast.

Study the Sample

Read the steps below to see what the writer considered as he developed his compare-and-contrast paragraph.

Step 1: Picking a Topic. The writer decided to compare and contrast information from the graph "American Workers in Selected Occupations" on page 35.

Step 2: Developing and Organizing the Paragraph. Then the writer listed and organized facts from the graph and wrote a topic sentence.

What does the graph show?	Compare: Look for similarities	Contrast: Look for differences
the percentage of Americans working in agriculture in 1900 and 1994		sharp drop, from about 35% to less than 5% between 1900 and 1994
the percentage of Americans working in manufacturing, mining, and construction in 1900 and 1994	almost the same	
the percentage of Americans working in services in 1900 and 1994		sharp increase, from about 5% to about 25% between 1900 and 1994

Now read the compare-and-contrast paragraph. Then it will be your turn.

Your Turn

A. Prewriting

Step 1: You can compare and contrast data from the graph "Employment Status of Civilian Labor Force" on page 36, or choose a graph from another source.

Step 2: List and organize facts from the graph. Use the comparison and contrast chart on the next page if you like. Then write a topic sentence.

Occupational Changes in the U.S.

How have the occupations of Americans changed since the beginning of the 20th century? According to the U.S. Bureau of Labor Statistics, about 65 percent of American workers at the beginning of the 20th century selected occupations in agriculture; manufacturing, mining, and construction; or services such as business and repair services, personal services, professional and related services, and entertainment and recreation. The next 94 years saw the following changes: Agriculture, which employed more than a third of workers in 1900, was the chosen occupation of less than 5 percent by 1994. On the other hand, while only about 5 percent of working Americans were employed in services in 1900, almost 25 percent worked in those occupations in 1994. The percentage of Americans working in manufacturing, mining, and construction jobs remained about the same.

What does the graph show?	Compare: Look for similarities	Contrast: Look for differences
_____	_____	_____
_____	_____	_____
_____	_____	_____
_____	_____	_____
_____	_____	_____
_____	_____	_____
_____	_____	_____

Write a topic sentence for your paragraph here.

_____

Tip After you have organized your points of comparison and contrast, write a sentence that states the general topic of the graph. That will help direct your writing.

B. Writing

On separate paper write a paragraph comparing and contrasting the data.

 Save your draft. At the end of this unit, you will work with one of your drafts further.

▶ Writing Skills Mini-Lesson: Commonly Confused Words

There are many words that sound the same or almost the same as other English words. When you write, you need to know how to spell and use these sound-alike words. Here are a few of the most commonly confused words.

1. *Your* and *you're*
   your—a possessive word meaning "belonging to you"
   > Do you like **your** job in the factory?
   you're—a contraction of *you are*
   > **You're** working too hard. = **You are** working too hard.

2. *Its* and *it's*
   its—a possessive word meaning "belonging to it"
   > That machine seems to have a mind of **its** own.
   it's—a contraction of *it is*
   > **It's** hard to work the night shift. = **It is** hard to work the night shift.

3. *Whose* and *who's*
   whose—a possessive word meaning "belonging to whom"
   > **Whose** job is it, anyway?
   who's—a contraction of *who is* or *who has*
   > **Who's** going to repair the machine? = **Who is** going to repair the machine?
   > **Who's** found the instructions? = **Who has** found the instructions?

4. *There, their,* and *they're*
   there—a word used to introduce a sentence; a word meaning "in that place."
   > **There** should be glue in the storeroom. Look **there** again.
   their—a possessive word meaning "belonging to them"
   > **Their** jobs pay pretty well.
   they're—a contraction of *they are*
   > **They're** working in the factory. = **They are** working in the factory.

Remember: Use an apostrophe to form a contraction. Do not use an apostrophe to form the possessive of pronouns.

Practice: Look at the words in parentheses. On separate paper, copy each sentence, writing the correct word in each blank.
1. (Whose, Who's) _____ the hardest-working person you know?
2. (There, Their, They're) _____ are different kinds of work: paid and unpaid.
3. (whose, who's) A homemaker and a factory worker both work, but _____ job is harder?
4. (There, Their, They're) _____ both hard jobs with _____ own demands.
5. (your, you're) When you take care of _____ children, _____ working hard.
6. (your, you're) If you work in a factory, _____ also working hard, but _____ earning money.
7. (Its, It's) _____ different for homemakers.
8. (there, their, they're) A well-run home and a happy family are _____ rewards.

Unit 1 Review

Reading Review

Occupational Wage Survey

This bar graph shows wages for various clerical occupations in Illinois in 1996. The entry-level wage is the hourly rate earned when a clerk with no experience starts work. The median wage is the wage in the middle. The number of workers earning more than the median wage equals the number earning less than the median wage.

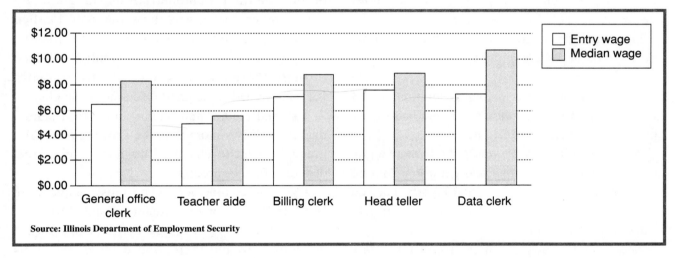

Source: Illinois Department of Employment Security

Choose the best answer to each question.

1. The clerical occupation with the highest entry-level hourly wage is
   (1) general office clerk (3) head teller
   (2) billing clerk (4) data clerk

2. The clerical position that shows the greatest increase in the hourly wage between entry-level and median is
   (1) general office clerk (3) head teller
   (2) teacher aide (4) data clerk

3. In general, the lowest paid clerical position at both the entry level and median wage is
   (1) general office clerk (3) billing clerk
   (2) teacher aide (4) data clerk

4. Which of the following statements best summarizes the information on the graph?
   (1) The wages of teacher aides show very little increase from entry level to median.
   (2) Data clerks earn more money than other clerks at all levels.
   (3) Entry-level wages for clerical occupations cluster around $6 an hour, but the range of median wages is much wider.
   (4) Most entry-level clerks earn between $6 and $8 an hour, but most other clerks earn at least $8 an hour.

Ike Mazo

Studs Terkel

In his book *The Great Divide: Second Thoughts on the American Dream,* Studs Terkel has recorded his interviews with Americans from all walks of life. The following selection is an interview in which a working-class father, Ike Mazo, talks about himself, his life, and his work.

Cliff's son. He is thirty-six. With his wife and three sons, fifteen, thirteen, and twelve, he lives in an archetypal[1] Chicago neighborhood: bungalow, blue-collar.

The mailbox reads: Mazo-Dudak: a new phenomenon in this community.

This is the first time in four generations that I have it worse than my father. My father had steady employment when he wanted it.

You had a thirty-, forty-year period where a guy could come in off the street and get a job. And go on. There were always strikes and layoffs, but you always came back. You could plan your life financially. You could say, I'll take X amount of income and I'll buy a house. I can put away X amount of income, so I could send at least one of my kids to college.

That's changed for me. My wife has went to work. Income-wise, we're the same. Standard of living, we're not. My father had hospital benefits. He was paid something while he was off sick. We pay our own hospitalization, what little we have. If I break my leg right now, we're gonna lose this house.

I went into the Marine Corps at seventeen, I came out at nineteen. I volunteered, of course. Came out of that, all screwed up mentally. It wasn't what I expected. A seventeen-year-old kid had been exposed to combat films and glory and stuff such as that: everything you had been brought up with. I swallowed all of it: George Washington, cherry tree, and everything. You come out and it's all gone.

You always felt that this country could do no wrong. We were always the good guys, whoever we take on are the bad guys. I was pro-Vietnam, I was one hundred percent. It was really funny, because I came home and my father was involved in anti-Vietnam demonstrations (laughs). My twin brother, Mike, was the same way. I called him a hippie. He was workin' in the mills, but he was goin' to college at night. I wanted to sweep through there and kick ass, get it over with, get out. We had some good discussions (laughs).

I started readin' and readin' in depth. I started readin' the news more than the sporting page. You gradually start to change. Plus there was a great deal of influence around.

I got out at nineteen, when most people were bein' drafted. Prior to Vietnam, I wanted to go to college. For two or three years after I came back, I got jobs here and there, and made a conscious decision to be a worker.

I was walkin' by Southworks, U.S. Steel, and saw the sign: HELP WANTED. This is 1972. You can literally walk across the street and get a job. So I got an apprenticeship as a boilermaker. That's what I am now, a journeyman boilermaker. The main reason I stayed at Southworks was the satisfaction in bein' a griever. You know, the one people come to when they have grievances. That was the greatest experience in the world. Up until this time, you're a worker and they're the boss. They have no problem pointin' that out to you damn near every day. I would sit in there as a high school dropout and I'm up against this college-educated superintendent, and you're on one-and-one and you're as good as him.

1. **archetypal** (ar/ki/TIE/pul) relating to a model or perfect example of something

My father didn't want me in the mills. He cussed me and my brother both. Said he fought for twenty years to stay out of the mills, and me and my brother were lookin' at it simply as a job. You had to have a job.

I would want my children to go to college. But I never shared that idea that you strive and work and struggle so your children can rise above your class, which is working-class. If they choose that, so be it. I don't know if my father wanted me to be a doctor, lawyer, but—I wouldn't want my kids in the mill.

What do I see for my kids? I really don't know. It's kind of frightening, scary. It's not only for my kids. It's that whole young group. You get enough of 'em out of work and those are the ones that'll trip across the picket line. If they've never worked, they don't have that tradition. They've never worked with that old guy next to 'em.

I had a very close friend who went across the *Tribune* picket line. What do I do? I go shun this guy? Don't have nothin' to do with him? My father said, Yeah, cut him off.

I don't think this guy will ever do it again. When we bought this house, I had a little get-together. He didn't wanna come. He was ashamed. I remember him tellin' me, "You're treatin' me like a piece of shit." I said, "What do you expect? If they break that strike and you're gonna be permanent there, they'll want your head right. They don't care about you."

When you come back from Vietnam, you're angry, chip on your shoulder. You go to work and you start gettin' treated a certain way. . . . So you try different things. I was gonna be so good at my job that no boss was ever gonna mess with me. Then you realize that's not the answer. Look what happened at Southworks. The logical answer is havin' unions, all around you. These young kids figure the time for a union has come and went. They figure they can make it on their own. Individualism and makin' it on your own is an admirable trait. But it don't work that way. They

never had the one older guy tellin' the next guy come along what it's all about.

Why did Southworks close? U.S. Steel bought Marathon Oil. And they was gettin' millions of dollars every time they shut down a facility. They had until April to shut us down to get the writeoff for the previous year.

This was one of the most modern facilities around. They got caster there, they got electric furnace, they got the oxygen process. And thousands of guys were laid off. So how's the individual gonna make it on his own? When the mill closed down in '82, I was out of work for a year and a half. That's when my wife went to work. The kids are old enough, she likes her job. Even if I make considerably less at my new job—just got it five days ago—it's gonna be two incomes.

This new job is a real pain. I'm hopin' they lay me off in thirty days.

I'm a journeyman with fourteen years experience. They're treatin' me like a dog. The reason I became a craftsman was for a certain amount of dignity. They don't want craftsmen at this place, they want animals. How they're gonna treat these kids that are goin' out there, I don't know.

I've heard it many a time. Them people don't wanna work. There's jobs out there for six dollars an hour and they won't take 'em. When I was in high school, they told you: Go out, work hard, make something of your life. Now they're tellin' you you're not a good citizen if you're not willing to accept less. The whole country's supposed to accept less. It's steadily comin' down. It's an attack on the living standard of workers, since Reagan. And the best way is to hit the unions.

I'm workin' harder, makin' less money, got less of a future. I was put outa work in the steel mills at the ideal age. With ten years in the work force, still in my thirties, that's the guy they wanna hire. But now I'm pushin' forty. I know the law says they're supposed to do it, but they just don't hire you. This guy I know is gonna be forty-five, great skills and work history—just went back at a plant— maintenance. My wife is working. Friends of mine have problems with it. That guy that crossed the picket line. He didn't have to do it, he wasn't that hard up. He was right there with me in the union. . . . But I know he felt low being at home. He felt it was a reflection on him. He's Mexican.

His pride, his macho.

There's somethin' in my life I always wanted to do. I'd like to be a cabinetmaker. I'm makin' a table there. Before I die, I would like to make somethin' and stick it in the window and say, "I made this. If I sell it, I sell it. If I don't, I don't. But what I've made has never been made before."

Choose the best answer to each question.

5. One way that Ike's life is different from his father's is that Ike
(1) has little financial security
(2) graduated from high school
(3) is not proud of his work
(4) receives better hospitalization and other benefits

6. One way that Ike's life is similar to his father's is that both
(1) had working wives
(2) changed careers in midlife
(3) did not want their children to work in the mills
(4) supported the war in Vietnam

7. Ike liked being a griever with the union because he
(1) was troubled on his return from Vietnam
(2) was angry that his friend crossed a picket line
(3) could get away with having a chip on his shoulder
(4) was on equal standing with his college-educated boss

8. Each of the following terms characterizes Ike Mazo *except*
(1) pro-union
(2) lazy
(3) disillusioned
(4) resentful

The Writing Process

In Unit 1, you wrote three first drafts. Choose the piece that you would like to work with further. You will revise, edit, and make a final copy of this draft.
____ your character sketch of someone you know on page 22
____ your poem about your own work experience on page 32
____ your paragraph comparing and contrasting the data from a graph on page 40

Find the first draft you chose. Then turn to page 176 in this book. Follow steps 3, 4, and 5 in the Writing Process to create a final draft.

As you revise, check your draft for these specific points:

Character sketch: Be sure you described at least three clear examples of the character traits you chose.

Poem: Make sure the words you used to describe the people, places, objects, and details work together to create a certain feeling or mood.

Compare-and-contrast paragraph: Be sure you compared and contrasted key facts on the graph and opened your paragraph with a statement or question introducing its topic.

Unit 2 Breaking New Ground

People who break new ground are people who do something for the first time. In your personal life, you break new ground when you try something new. At work, people break new ground in many ways: when they are the first to do a new job, or first to do a job in a new and better way, or first to stand up for their rights as workers.

In this unit, you will read about an up-and-coming African American banker trying to break new ground at a business lunch. You will learn about a law that broke new ground for working people with disabilities. And you will read about the experiences of a woman breaking into a "man's job."

Before you begin Unit 2, think about the kind of person who breaks new ground so that others can follow. Have you ever known such a person? Are you such a person yourself?

▶ **Be an Active Reader**

As you read the selections in this unit
- Put a question mark (?) by things you do not understand.
- <u>Underline</u> words you do not know. Try to use context clues to figure them out.

After you read each selection in this unit
- Reread sections you marked with a question mark. If they still do not make sense, discuss them with a partner or your instructor.
- Look at words you <u>underlined</u>. Discuss any words you still don't understand with a partner or your instructor, or look them up in a dictionary.

Lesson 4

LEARNING GOALS

Strategy: Use context clues
Reading: Read an excerpt from fiction
Skill: Make inferences
Writing: Write a personal narrative

Before You Read

This lesson's reading selection is a chapter from the novel *Brothers and Sisters* by Bebe Moore Campbell. In it you will read about Humphrey Boone, a man trying to gain acceptance in a group that has long excluded people like him. Consider times when *you* felt like an outsider trying to get in. Check any situations below that you have been in.

_____ **1.** Making friends in a new community
_____ **2.** Starting a new job
_____ **3.** Going to a party attended by people you don't know
_____ **4.** Participating in a church function for the first time
_____ **5.** Going to your first meeting of a group, organization, or club
_____ **6.** Being in the minority—due to age, race, or gender—in a group or organization

Think about how you felt as an outsider. How do you think the character in this story might feel?

_____

_____

Preview the Reading

Read the introduction to get a general idea about what is happening in the story. Look at the illustrations for impressions of the characters and their surroundings.

Set Your Strategy: Use Context Clues

Context clues are the words and sentences around an unfamiliar word. You can use context clues to figure out the meanings of unfamiliar words as you read. If you come across an unfamiliar word while reading this selection, try to use the context to figure out its meaning. Decide what word would make sense in that sentence. When you finish reading, you will have a chance to choose words and phrases that define some words from the story.

Brothers and Sisters is set in Los Angeles in 1992. In the following excerpt, Humphrey Boone, an African American businessman, is the guest of Preston Sinclair, the president of the company Boone works for. They are having lunch at Sinclair's almost all-white private club.

from Brothers and Sisters

Bebe Moore Campbell

Preston and Humphrey walked the block to the penthouse restaurant, part of the La Jolla[1] Club, Preston's private club. The early spring weather was cool, and the sun was bright; Humphrey was grateful for the crisp air. Between coming into the bank on weekends, working on the private placement deals he was trying to set up, and trying to put out the fires that constantly raged in the lives of his family, he hadn't had a chance to get out and enjoy himself. Now, as he felt the breezes against his cheek, he made a mental note to try to schedule a tennis game for the weekend.

Humphrey had been to the club before, but the elegance of the turn-of-the-century architecture, the opulence of the dark, rich mahogany-paneled walls, the beauty of the heavy Oriental rugs, the lushness of the huge urns filled with exotic flowers, the richness of the rare paintings and tapestries that covered the walls, the deference of the staff, with their Yessirs, Nosirs, and quick smiles, were always impressive.

1. **La Jolla** (lah/HOY/yah)

Preston introduced him to several of the distinguished-looking gentlemen who were having drinks at the bar in the corner of the room. Humphrey saw two board members from his previous bank. He tapped them on their backs, and when the men turned around and saw him, their eyes contained the startled, almost frightened looks that Humphrey knew so well. He could have predicted that surprise and fear, yet both still had the power to offend and enrage him. But he smiled quickly, extended his hand, and said, "Humphrey Boone," and the light of recognition immediately displaced the fear as the unknown black man and possible assailant became someone they knew, someone safe. They clapped him heartily on his back and declared how wonderful it was to see him, and then Humphrey took them over and introduced them to Preston. They chatted for a few minutes, lacing their farewells with such sincere goodwill that Humphrey almost forgave them. Almost.

White folks sure know how to live, he said to himself, as he glanced around the magnificent lobby. For of course, the hallowed halls of the La Jolla Club were for all practical purposes the almost exclusive province of white males, although immediately after the civil unrest of April 29, the first black member, the owner of a chain of parking lots throughout the city, was inducted. But as Humphrey seated himself at a table in the penthouse restaurant, he was very much aware, as was everyone else in the club, that he was the only black person in the room, other than two rather decrepit[2] waiters.

"This is the best place in the city for veal," Preston said, as both men looked out the window next to their table. Below them the people appeared to Humphrey like so many bright specks, jewels set into a gigantic, sparkling pendant. But instead of seeing people, Preston saw his son's swollen, bruised face. He saw his son hobbling on one limb, dragging his injured leg as he grimaced and groaned. Preston drew his hand to his mouth and bit down on his index finger. He looked over at Humphrey, who was staring at him uneasily. "So," Preston said a bit too loudly, "I've been hearing great things about you. Tell me about the private placement deals you've lined up."

Humphrey leaned slightly forward and peered at Preston. On the several occasions when he'd been with the president, he was usually on guard, monitoring his language, gestures, and references, making sure that he didn't offend in any way. He was careful not to say anything that could be construed as angry, belligerent, or militant, because that kind of behavior, even a hint of it, made white folks nervous. Humphrey was tuned in to every smile and facial tic of the powerful white man he was with, because his survival depended upon his clear-sighted interpretation of everything that crossed Preston Sinclair's mind.

Looking at the president, Humphrey realized that something was slightly off. The few times he'd been with Preston, he filled the room with his bigger-than-life energy. The man sitting across

from him seemed shrunken somehow.

Preston could feel the younger man's enthusiasm as he launched into a neat rundown of the many aspects of the deals he'd created. "The beauty of it is that I've already got several insurance companies lined up. They're all anxious to participate; it's just a matter of getting the right terms."

"I understand that the terms will be quite lucrative for Angel City," Preston said.

"If things go the way I think they should, we're looking at approximately one point seven million dollars' profit. More importantly, these deals will put Angel City squarely up front with the rest of the players in the private placement market. They serve to put everyone on notice that there's a new kid on the block. And, Mr. Sinclair, I want you to know that your reputation makes my job so much easier." The praise slid off his tongue easily, but his tone reflected the sincerity that propelled it. He had to admit that Preston Sinclair was well connected and highly respected.

Preston heard the compliment, but he couldn't feel it. "Thank you," he said. He started to say that he was pleased to have Humphrey on the Angel City team, but he hesitated. He didn't want to sound paternalistic.[3] They didn't like that. Just as he was about to speak, an attendant appeared and handed him a cellular phone. "There's a call for you, Mr. Sinclair."

Humphrey said, "I'll just excuse myself," and began to stand. Preston motioned for him to sit down. Cupping his hand over the receiver, he said, "This will just be a minute, I'm sure." But then Claire came on the telephone, and she was crying.

"Darling, what's wrong?"

In the midst of her loud wailing, he heard the word "surgery." Everything around him went hazy.

Humphrey watched as Preston's cheeks began to sag and his eyes stared straight ahead without focusing on anything. Again he started to rise. This time he felt Preston's fingers grip his wrist. One

---

2. **decrepit** (di/KREH/pit) weakened by old age

3. **paternalistic** (puh/TER/nuhl/IS/tik) treating others as a father treats his children

look in his hollow eyes, and Humphrey knew that it was the act of a blind man, reaching out for something steady.

"Calm down," Preston said. "Calm down, darling." He was aware of movement across the table from him, but everything and everyone around him had become dim. For a moment, he couldn't catch his breath or speak. He had a sense of holding on to something. "What are you saying? What are you saying?"

But Claire could only sob out a jumbled response that he couldn't comprehend. She was hysterical. He knew that she wanted him to come home, but she wouldn't ask him. He felt guilty for not offering.

"All right. All right," he said. He didn't ask pertinent, pointed questions but allowed himself to get caught up completely in his wife's frenzied emotions, which wasn't his style. Emotions didn't make good business sense. Not at all. But above all

else, he wanted Claire to stop crying. I should leave, he thought, just go home. But his body seemed frozen. He was afraid to go home. Scared of what he'd find. Frightened of what it might mean to become a man who went home in the middle of a business day just because his wife was crying. "You'll be all right, darling. Have a cup of tea. Stop crying." When he switched off the telephone, he still felt as though he were with her, and it took a full minute for his heart to calm down, for everything around him to come into clear focus, and when it did, he realized that his fingers were wrapped tightly around Humphrey Boone's wrist. "I'm sorry," Preston said, withdrawing his hand. "I . . . uh . . . where were we?"

"Are you all right, Mr. Sinclair?" Humphrey asked. His wrist felt a little sore where Preston had squeezed it. Preston looked pale and suddenly much older, really haggard. Humphrey had never noticed the deep circles under his eyes before. Droplets of perspiration were collecting near his hairline. His gaze seemed to be focused at some point in space. When he looked into the white man's eyes, Humphrey saw trouble etched in the creases around his eyes, in the sharp deep line between his eyebrows, the kind of trouble he'd been raised on. "Are you all right?" he repeated. The man looked as if he could have a heart attack at any minute.

"No," Preston said, "I'm not." He sighed wearily. It was the middle of a workday and he was conducting business and his cardinal[4] rule was never to discuss personal matters at work. If the truth be told, Preston rarely engaged in an intimate conversation. "My son, the older boy, Pres, was hurt badly in a car accident several weeks ago. He almost died." Preston spoke haltingly, as though the words he was speaking were coming through a pipe that was rusty from disuse. As he began to speak, he realized that except for Claire and Robbie and the doctors, he hadn't discussed his

4. cardinal (KARD/nul) most important; chief

son's medical condition with anyone. "He was in a hospital back East for a while before we brought him home for physical therapy. It's not going well. My wife is very upset. She was always so self-sufficient." He said that last as though the very idea of Claire being needy was a concept he couldn't quite grasp.

"It's not every day your child almost dies," Humphrey said, hoping he was saying the correct thing. He smiled sympathetically. "I'm sure he'll be all right. He's young. How old?"

"Twenty-two."

"At that age, they still have Jell-O for bones. He'll mend. When I was twenty-four, I broke my back. I was painting the second floor of my mother's house, and I fell off the ladder. They told my mother that I'd be in a body cast for six months. I was out in less than three and back on the basketball team in four. Did he play sports in school?"

Preston hesitated. The balls of his son's childhood, small and white, orangy pigskin, round and hard, whizzed back and forth across his mind, but he couldn't place them. They were just so many catches, passes, and baskets that he'd never seen played, so many games missed. His mind fastened on the hard white ball. "He plays tennis very well. He's on his college team. He talked about becoming pro, although frankly we discouraged that."

"Then he's in shape. Being in shape counts a lot when the body is trying to heal. He'll be all right."

"I haven't seen him play tennis in a long time," Preston blurted out. The words seemed to accuse him of something. He lowered his head. "I missed a lot of his games when he was growing up. His mother went," he said in a barely audible voice.

The two of them were silent. A thin Latino waiter came over, but Humphrey waved him away. He didn't know how to read the president's sudden personal revelations.[5] He still seemed pale and strangely lethargic.[6] "Well, my mom was the one who came to my games too," he said smoothly. He added, "My dad was, uh, too busy working."

Preston searched Humphrey's face. "Did you hold that against him?"

"No," Humphrey said quickly. "He had to make the money. I understood that. He made sure that my sisters and brother and I had everything that we needed. We never wanted for anything." When Humphrey tried to swallow, his throat was sore, as though the words had scraped it raw.

"My father wasn't around much either," Preston said, "although his absence didn't result in material comforts for our family. He was a minister. Always out and about, doing good. Every Saturday morning, he wrote his sermon. In the spring and summer, when he was finished, he'd take us kids for ice cream. When it was cold, we'd go for hot chocolate. Boy, we were a happy little band of ragamuffins." Preston's laughter rose like the notes of a trombone and then faded. Humphrey watched as he stared off into space. "My God," Preston said. "We had absolutely nothing, and we didn't even know it."

"When it's really nothing, you know it," Humphrey said, and instantly regretted his words. He knew he sounded bitter and angry. He tried to cover up his emotions with a smile so broad that he thought his lips were going to crack.

But Preston seemed too lost in thought to have even heard his words, let alone picked up the tone. "We lived in a very small town in Indiana. Parkerville. The entire business district was only two blocks. The drugstore where we got the ice cream and hot chocolate was on Main Street. Parsons' Drugstore." Preston let out a laugh. "We made quite a little procession going down the street. Every few feet, someone would stop and greet my father. Everyone knew Reverend Sinclair. He was so well respected. People loved him."

---

5. **revelations** (reh/vuh/LAY/shuns) things made known

6. **lethargic** (le/THAR/jik) drowsy; sluggish

"Preachers' kids are usually pretty wild, aren't they?"

"In a town of forty-five hundred people, it's hard to sow wild oats. That had to wait until I left for school, but yes, I did make up for lost time."

"Do you get back home much?" Humphrey asked, interrupting Preston's reverie.[7]

"No. My parents are deceased. My brothers and sisters are scattered all over. I haven't been back in years. I should have taken the boys back there more often," he said. "They visited when they were small, but when we moved out here, they stopped going. I should have kept the connections stronger. They don't know their roots."

"Well," Humphrey said, "it's never too late to find your roots."

They both chuckled a little. The two separate sounds knotted together as tightly as a handshake.

Preston's shoulders eased down a bit, and he let his jaw muscles go slack. "Your son will be fine," Humphrey said, and the white man nodded his head.

"When Pres is better, I'd like you to come by the house and meet him," Preston said. "I'll have my secretary call you with a date."

Humphrey was silent, as he felt the full weight of what he'd just heard. An invitation to dinner was an offer to be molded and groomed, mentored and befriended. Preston Sinclair was asking to be his friend. There was no mistaking his intent. And he

wasn't asking in a calculated manner but in a moment of sincerity and vulnerability.[8] Preston Sinclair had anointed[9] him again. For the first time, it occurred to Humphrey that the man might be serious about helping him become the first black president of a major bank. Preston Sinclair just might be a man he could trust.

7. **reverie** (REH/vuh/ree) dreamy thoughts

8. **vulnerability** (vul/neh/ruh/BI/li/tee) a condition of being too exposed, unprotected

9. **anointed** (uh/NOIN/ted) chosen for something special by someone in power

Choose the word or phrase that means the same as the **bold** word in each line from the story.

1. ". . . the **opulence** of the dark, rich mahogany-paneled walls . . ."
   (1) dreariness   (3) lushness
   (2) dullness   (4) woodenness

2. "the **deference** of the staff, with their Yessirs, Nosirs, and quick smiles . . ."
   (1) respectfulness   (3) inference
   (2) patience   (4) pleasantness

3. ". . . dragging his injured leg as he **grimaced** and groaned . . ."
   (1) had a patient look
   (2) made a moaning sound
   (3) walked with a limp
   (4) made a pained expression

4. "He was careful not to say anything that could be **construed** as angry. . . ."
   (1) remembered   (3) overheard
   (2) understood   (4) mispronounced

5. ". . . construed as angry, **belligerent**, or militant, because that kind of behavior . . . made white folks nervous"
   (1) excited   (3) fearless
   (2) quarrelsome   (4) hateful

6. "'. . . the terms will be quite **lucrative**' . . . 'approximately one point seven million dollars' profit.'"
   (1) profitable   (3) acceptable
   (2) reasonable   (4) desirable

After You Read

A. Comprehension Check

1. Humphrey Boone works for a
   (1) tennis club
   (2) church
   (3) restaurant
   (4) bank

2. When Preston Sinclair had business meetings, his cardinal rule was that he
   (1) always ate first and then talked about business
   (2) never accepted telephone calls from his wife
   (3) never discussed his personal life
   (4) always met in a place where he would be noticed

3. Preston Sinclair learns from his wife that
   (1) his son needs surgery
   (2) young Pres would never again play tennis
   (3) his sons want to visit their father's childhood home
   (4) their son was in a car accident

4. By the end of the excerpt, Humphrey believes that Preston Sinclair
   (1) will do something to make him quit his job
   (2) will never be a friend to him
   (3) lived a worse childhood than Humphrey did
   (4) will help him in his career

5. The La Jolla Club had allowed an African American businessman to join
   (1) because the courts had ordered them to
   (2) to help calm racial tension in the city
   (3) because the businessman had many friends in the club
   (4) because the businessman paid to be allowed in

6. When the author writes that Preston "didn't want to sound paternalistic. They didn't like that," we know that Preston is all of the following *except*
   (1) unsure of himself around African Americans
   (2) sensitive to other people's feelings
   (3) prejudiced against African Americans
   (4) anxious not to offend Humphrey

B. Read between the Lines

Check each statement that is likely to be true based on evidence from the story. Do not check statements that have no evidence to support them.

_____ **1.** Humphrey is capable and effective at his job.
_____ **2.** Young Pres's accident has changed his mother.
_____ **3.** Being poor as a boy made Preston want to be rich when he grew up.
_____ **4.** Humphrey grew up in a well-to-do family.
_____ **5.** Humphrey and Preston respect each other.
_____ **6.** Humphrey is highly ambitious.

C. Think beyond the Reading

Discuss these questions with a partner. Answer them in writing on separate paper if you wish.

1. In what ways is Humphrey breaking new ground? Do African Americans still have such experiences today? What are your reasons for your answer?

2. Think about each experience you noted in Before You Read on page 48. Did you gain acceptance into the groups you checked? Why or why not?

Think About It: Make Inferences

When you answered the questions in Read between the Lines on page 55, you were **making inferences.** Authors seldom explain everything when writing fiction. Instead, they give hints and clues through their characters' thoughts and actions and the carefully chosen details they include. It is up to the reader to **infer,** or figure out, those things that are not actually stated. To **make an inference,** you use the details in a story plus your own knowledge and understanding. The author of *Brothers and Sisters* gives you many details that you can combine with what you already know to infer things about the characters in the chapter.

A. Look at Making Inferences

Reread the following excerpt from *Brothers and Sisters* to look for details that you can use to make inferences.

> ▶ Humphrey saw two board members from his previous bank. He tapped them on their backs, and when the men turned around and saw him, their eyes contained the startled, almost frightened looks that Humphrey knew so well. He could have predicted that surprise and fear, yet both still had the power to offend and enrage him. But he smiled quickly, extended his hand, and said, "Humphrey Boone," and the light of recognition immediately displaced the fear as the unknown black man and possible assailant became someone they knew, someone safe.

The chart below shows how story details and knowledge about the world can help you make inferences while you read.

Story Details	What You Already Know	Inferences
• The board members had startled, almost frightened looks. • The unknown black man and possible assailant became someone safe.	• Some white people are prejudiced against black people. • Some white people fear black people and think they are dangerous.	• The board members were white. They were surprised to see a black man in their private club. • They may be afraid of black men they don't know, perhaps because they fear being attacked by them.

What could you infer from the detail "looks that Humphrey knew so well"?

_____

_____

You know that many African Americans have faced the prejudice of others. You can infer that Humphrey has met with this same kind of prejudice before.

When you read something you don't quite understand, ask yourself, "What have I seen or heard that would explain what I just read?" Use your experience to help you make inferences.

B. Practice

Reread these excerpts from the novel, noting the details and adding your knowledge to them to make inferences about the characters and events. Then check all the inferences you can make. After each inference you check, note details from the excerpt above it that explain why you can make that inference.

1. ▶ Humphrey leaned slightly forward and peered at Preston. On the several occasions when he'd been with the president, he was usually on guard, monitoring his language, gestures, and references, making sure that he didn't offend in any way. He was careful not to say anything that could be construed as angry, belligerent, or militant, because that kind of behavior, even a hint of it, made white folks nervous.

_____ **a.** Humphrey has a fairly high position in the bank. _____

_____ **b.** Humphrey was nearsighted. _____

_____ **c.** Humphrey felt uncomfortable with Preston. _____

_____ **d.** Humphrey was prejudiced against white people. _____

2. ▶ "I haven't seen him play tennis in a long time," Preston blurted out. The words seemed to accuse him of something. He lowered his head. "I missed a lot of his games when he was growing up. His mother went," he said in a barely audible voice.

_____ **a.** Preston is almost blind. _____

_____ **b.** Preston put his work before his family. _____

_____ **c.** Young Pres hasn't played tennis in a long time. _____

_____ **d.** Preston feels guilty and embarrassed. _____

_____ **e.** Preston is losing his voice. _____

> ▶ **Talk About It**
> As a black man trying to gain social and professional acceptance in the white business community, Humphrey Boone monitors his language, gestures, and references. He wants to make sure he doesn't offend anyone. With a partner, pick an experience from the list in Before You Read on page 48. Make a list of do's and don'ts for people who are breaking new ground in a social or work setting. Discuss your list with the class.

Write About It: Write a Personal Narrative

A **narrative** tells a story. In *Brothers and Sisters,* the author tells the story of an African American man's struggle to be accepted into the white business world. Now you will have a chance to write a personal narrative about a time you felt like an outsider and whether or not you were eventually accepted. First, study the sample, which shows how to write a personal narrative.

Study the Sample

Read the steps below to see how the writer developed her personal narrative.

Step 1: Picking a Topic. In the sample narrative, the writer describes being a new member in the Parent-Teacher Association (PTA).

Step 2: Developing and Organizing the Narrative. The writer used the story map below to list and organize details for her narrative.

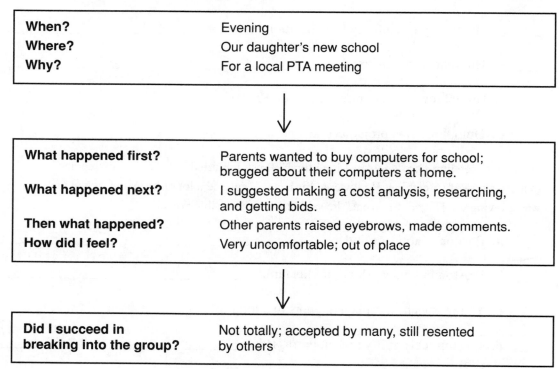

When?	Evening
Where?	Our daughter's new school
Why?	For a local PTA meeting

What happened first?	Parents wanted to buy computers for school; bragged about their computers at home.
What happened next?	I suggested making a cost analysis, researching, and getting bids.
Then what happened?	Other parents raised eyebrows, made comments.
How did I feel?	Very uncomfortable; out of place

| Did I succeed in breaking into the group? | Not totally; accepted by many, still resented by others |

Now read her personal narrative on the next page. Then it will be your turn.

Your Turn

A. Prewriting

Step 1: You may write about one of the topics below or choose a topic of your own.

- starting a new job
- attending a new school
- a group or organization you joined
- a party where you didn't know anyone

Breaking into the PTA

When my daughter entered first grade, I went back to work full-time. But I wanted to be more involved in her education than just helping her with her homework at night. So there I was, attending my first Parent-Teacher Association meeting.

The president called the group to order. First on the agenda was the PTA's purchase of computers for the children's classrooms. I sat for three-quarters of an hour, listening to parents brag about the computers their children used at home. They even compared notes on the computer games their kids liked to play. Finally, I raised my hand and stood up. "Hi! I think you should develop a cost analysis for your computer purchases," I said.

"Pardon me?" asked the president, a little taken aback.

"I work in the purchasing department of my company. Computers and computer supplies can be quite costly, so we'll want to get bids from several different vendors. And new technology is developing rapidly, so we'll need to research which computers are most likely to be relevant three or four years from now. Right?"

I couldn't believe the raised eyebrows. I heard comments such as, "Who is she, anyway?" and "Who does she think she is?" I felt like I had stumbled into a beehive. I've never been so uncomfortable in my life.

After more discussion, some of the members started accepting my ideas. A group was formed to research and evaluate the latest computer hardware and educational software. Another group was formed to request bids from area vendors. Eventually, most of the other PTA members started accepting me too. But I still feel resented by some. I learned the hard way to ease my way into a new group a little more slowly and a little less forcefully.

State your topic here.

_____

Step 2: On separate paper, organize your details. If you like, make a story map like the one on page 58.

B. Writing

Now on separate paper, write about the topic you selected.

Tip When you write a personal narrative, arrange the events in the order in which they happened. Then add details that explain each event and help your reader picture what happened.

▶ **Save your draft.** At the end of this unit, you will work with one of your drafts further.

Lesson 5

LEARNING GOALS

Strategy: Use your background knowledge
Reading: Read a brochure
Skill: Apply information
Writing: Write a fact sheet

Before You Read

A person with a disability is someone who has a physical or mental condition that seriously limits the ability to walk, see, hear, breathe, learn, or work. Before the Americans with Disabilities Act of 1990, many people with such conditions were denied jobs and job promotions because of their disabilities. The brochure in this lesson, "The Americans with Disabilities Act: Your Employment Rights as an Individual with a Disability," explains those workers' civil rights established by the act.

Before you read the brochure, think about people with disabilities in the workplace. Check each question that you think the brochure might answer.

_____ **1.** Does the Americans with Disabilities Act guarantee equal opportunity to people with disabilities?

_____ **2.** Can employers refuse to hire qualified people with disabilities?

_____ **3.** Must a store put price labels in Braille for blind customers?

_____ **4.** Can employers ask about a person's disability during a job interview?

_____ **5.** Who should people with disabilities contact if they believe an employer is discriminating against them?

Are there any other questions you think might be answered in the brochure? If so, write them below and look for the answers as you read.

_____

_____

Preview the Reading

Read the title and headings to find out what topics are covered. Read the headings and the *italic* type for key words and phrases.

Set Your Strategy: Use Your Background Knowledge

When you already know something about a topic, you can **use that background knowledge** to help you understand what you read. For example, to understand the following brochure, use what you know about people with disabilities, about the workplace, and about the rights of Americans in the workplace. When you finish, you will have a chance to identify the background knowledge that helped you understand what you read.

Since the early 1970s, many people with disabilities have fought for their rights to earn a living and to manage their daily activities. Their efforts have resulted in legislation in the U.S. that extends civil rights protection to Americans with disabilities. This brochure explains the rights in the workplace of people with disabilities.

The Americans with Disabilities Act

Your Employment Rights as an Individual with a Disability

U.S. Equal Employment Opportunity Commission

Introduction

The Americans with Disabilities Act of 1990 (ADA) makes it unlawful to discriminate[1] in employment against a qualified individual with a disability. The ADA also outlaws discrimination against individuals with disabilities in state and local government services, public accommodations,[2] transportation and telecommunications. This booklet explains the part of the ADA that prohibits job discrimination. This part of the law is enforced by the U.S. Equal Employment Opportunity Commission (EEOC) and state and local civil rights enforcement agencies that work with the Commission.

What Employers Are Covered by the ADA?

Job discrimination against people with disabilities is illegal if practiced by:

- private employers,
- state and local governments,
- employment agencies,
- labor organizations,
- and labor-management committees.

The part of the ADA enforced by the EEOC outlaws job discrimination by:

- all employers, including state and local government employers, with 25 or more employees after July 26, 1992, and
- all employers, including state and local government employers, with 15 or more employees after July 26, 1994.

Are You Protected by the ADA?

If you have a disability and are qualified to do a job, the ADA protects you from job discrimination on the basis of your disability.

---

1. **discriminate** (dis/KRIM/ih/nayt) treat a person or a group of people differently based on such factors as race, gender, national origin, etc.
2. **public accommodations** (a/KOM/uh/DAY/shuns) food, lodging, and other services available to the public

Under the ADA, you have a disability if you have a *physical or mental impairment*[3] that *substantially limits a major life activity*. The ADA also protects you if you have a history of such a disability, or if an employer believes that you have such a disability, even if you don't.

To be protected under the ADA, you must have, have a record of, or be regarded as having a *substantial*, as opposed to a minor, impairment. A substantial impairment is one that significantly limits or restricts a *major life activity* such as hearing, seeing, speaking, walking, breathing, performing manual tasks, caring for oneself, learning or working.

If you have a disability, you must also be qualified to perform the essential functions or duties of a job, with or without reasonable accommodation,[4] in order to be protected from job discrimination by the ADA. This means two things. First, you must satisfy the employer's requirements for the job, such as education, employment experience, skills or licenses. Second, you must be able to perform the *essential functions* of the job with or without *reasonable accommodation*. Essential functions are the fundamental job duties that you must be able to perform on your own or with the help of a reasonable accommodation. An employer cannot refuse to hire you because your disability prevents you from performing duties that are not essential to the job.

What Is Reasonable Accommodation?

Reasonable accommodation is any change or adjustment to a job or work environment that permits a qualified applicant or employee with a disability to participate in the job application process, to perform the essential functions of a job, or to enjoy benefits and privileges of employment equal to those enjoyed by employees without disabilities. For example, reasonable accommodation may include:

- providing or modifying equipment or devices,
- job restructuring,
- part-time or modified work schedules,
- reassignment to a vacant position,
- adjusting or modifying examinations, training materials, or policies,
- providing readers and interpreters, and
- making the workplace readily accessible to and usable by people with disabilities.

An employer is required to provide a reasonable accommodation to a qualified applicant or employee with a disability unless the employer can show that the accommodation would be an *undue hardship* —that is, that it would require significant difficulty or expense.

What Employment Practices Are Covered?

The ADA makes it unlawful to discriminate in all employment practices such as:

- recruitment
- hiring
- job assignments
- pay
- lay off
- firing
- training
- promotions
- benefits
- leave
- all other employment related activities.

It is also unlawful for an employer to retaliate against you for asserting your rights under the ADA. The Act also protects you if you are a victim of discrimination because of your family, business, social or other relationship or association with an individual with a disability.

---

3. impairment (im/PAIR/ment) injury; loss

4. accommodation adaptation or adjustment to settle differences

Can an Employer Require Medical Examinations or Ask Questions About a Disability?

If you are applying for a job, an employer cannot ask you if you are disabled or ask about the nature or severity of your disability. An employer can ask if you can perform the duties of the job with or without reasonable accommodation. An employer can also ask you to describe or to demonstrate how, with or without reasonable accommodation, you will perform the duties of the job.

An employer cannot require you to take a medical examination before you are offered a job. Following a job offer, an employer can condition the offer on your passing a required medical examination, but only if all entering employees for that job category have to take the examination. However, an employer cannot reject you because of information about your disability revealed by the medical examination, unless the reasons for rejection are job-related and necessary for the conduct of the employer's business. Nor can the employer refuse to hire you because of your disability if you can perform the essential functions of the job with an accommodation.

Once you have been hired and started work, your employer cannot require that you take a medical examination or ask questions about your disability unless they are related to your job and necessary for the conduct of your employer's business. Your employer may conduct voluntary medical examinations that are part of an employee health program, and may provide medical information required by state workers' compensation[5] laws to the agencies that administer such laws.

The results of all medical examinations must be kept confidential, and maintained in separate medical files.

Do Individuals Who Use Drugs Illegally Have Rights Under the ADA?

Anyone who is currently using drugs illegally is not protected by the ADA and may be denied employment or fired on the basis of such use. The ADA does not prevent employers from testing applicants or employees for current illegal drug use.

What Do I Do If I Think that I'm Being Discriminated Against?

If you think you have been discriminated against in employment on the basis of disability after July 26, 1992, you should contact the EEOC. A charge of discrimination generally must be filed within 180 days of the alleged[6] discrimination. You may have up to 300 days to file a charge if there is a state or local law that provides relief for discrimination on the basis of disability. However, to protect your rights, it is best to contact EEOC promptly if discrimination is suspected.

You may file a charge of discrimination on the basis of disability by contacting any EEOC field office, located in cities throughout the United States. If you have been discriminated against, you are entitled to a remedy that will place you in the position you would have been in if the discrimination had never occurred. You may be entitled to hiring, promotion, reinstatement, back pay, or reasonable accommodation, including reassignment. You may also be entitled to attorney's fees.

While the EEOC can only process ADA charges based on actions occurring on or after July 26, 1992, you may already be protected by state or local laws or by other current federal laws. EEOC field offices can refer you to the agencies that enforce those laws.

---

5. **workers' compensation** money paid to a worker injured on the job or made ill by working conditions
6. **alleged** (uh/LEJD) stated to be true, but not yet proven

To contact the nearest Equal Employment Opportunity Commission field office, call:
Phone: 1-800-669-4000
TDD: 1-800-669-6820

Can I Get Additional ADA Information and Assistance?

The EEOC will conduct an active technical assistance program to promote voluntary compliance[7] with the ADA. This program will be designed to help people with disabilities understand their rights and to help employers understand their responsibilities under the law.

In January 1992, EEOC will publish a Technical Assistance Manual,[8] providing practical application of legal requirements to specific employment activities, with a directory of resources to aid compliance. EEOC will publish other educational materials, provide training on the law for people with disabilities and for employers, and participate in meetings and training programs of other organizations. EEOC staff also will respond to individual requests for information and assistance. The Commission's technical assistance program will be separate and distinct from its enforcement responsibilities. Employers who seek information or assistance from the Commission will not be subject to any enforcement action because of such inquiries.

The Commission also recognizes that differences and disputes about ADA requirements may arise between employers and people with disabilities as a result of misunderstandings. Such disputes frequently can be resolved more effectively through informal negotiation or mediation procedures, rather than through the formal enforcement process of the ADA. Accordingly, EEOC will encourage efforts of employers and individuals with disabilities to settle such differences through alternative methods of dispute resolution, providing that such efforts do not deprive any individual of legal rights provided by the statute.

---

7. compliance (kum/PLY/ens) conforming to or coming into agreement with rules or practices
8. Several Technical Assistance Manuals and yearly supplements are available from the EEOC. Call the number above for information.

▶ **Revisit Your Strategy: Use Your Background Knowledge**

Use what you know about workplaces and about disabilities to explain the following quotations from the brochure.

1. What items and facilities have you seen in workplaces that make them "readily accessible to and usable by people with disabilities"?

_____

2. Although it is "unlawful for an employer to retaliate against you for asserting your rights under the ADA," how might employers retaliate against employees?

_____

After You Read

A. Comprehension Check

1. The ADA protects you from job discrimination if you
   (1) have a minor impairment
   (2) cannot do the job with reasonable accommodation
   (3) are disabled and are qualified for a job
   (4) use drugs illegally

2. An employer can require you to take a medical examination
   (1) at any time
   (2) before you are offered a job
   (3) to deduct medical expenses from your salary
   (4) after offering you a job if all new employees must take one

3. Employers must provide accommodation
   (1) unless it is too costly to be reasonable
   (2) until you can be laid off
   (3) unless you are in a wheelchair
   (4) even if you have no disability

4. If you believe you are discriminated against at work because of a disability, you should
   (1) quit the job immediately
   (2) file a charge of discrimination with the EEOC
   (3) pretend it never happened
   (4) take a medical examination

5. In the sentence ". . . you must have a . . . *substantial,* as opposed to a minor, impairment," *substantial* means
   (1) unimportant   (3) significant
   (2) imaginary   (4) dangerous

6. In the phrase "making the workplace readily *accessible,*" *accessible* means
   (1) able to be made safe
   (2) able to be inspected
   (3) able to be kept clean
   (4) able to be reached or used

B. Read between the Lines

Check the statements below that are true but not directly stated in the brochure.

_____ **1.** Federal government workers are not protected by the ADA.
_____ **2.** An employer can refuse to hire a secretary who needs crutches to walk even though the secretary has the training, education, and experience needed to do the job.
_____ **3.** Reasonable accommodation may include wheelchair access at doorways and in office hallways.
_____ **4.** An employer cannot fire you for filing a complaint with the EEOC.
_____ **5.** A person should tell about any accommodation needed when applying for a job.

C. Think beyond the Reading

Discuss these questions with a partner. Answer them in writing on separate paper if you wish.

1. Do you think the ADA goes far enough to guarantee people with disabilities the same opportunities to earn a living as other Americans? Why or why not?
2. Look at the questions you checked or wrote in Before You Read on page 60. Were they answered in the brochure? If not, where could you look for the answers?

Think About It: Apply Information

The purpose of the brochure "The Americans with Disabilities Act" is to give information about civil rights to people with disabilities and to employers. In order for the information in the brochure to be helpful, readers must be able to **apply the information.** (Remember that legal issues are complex. If you have actually faced discrimination because of a disability, you may want to consult a lawyer about the details of the case.)

A. Look at Applying Information

Read the case that follows. Then see how the ADA applies.

You are in a wheelchair and are interviewing for a position as an office receptionist. The employer tells you that the company is small with only 12 workers. She seems impressed with the training and skills you have described. But the employer telephones you the next day and tells you that she can't hire you because the receptionist sometimes needs to run errands. Can you file a charge of discrimination against the company?

Check each statement from the brochure that would help you to decide whether you can file a charge with the EEOC.

_____ **a.** Under the ADA, you have a disability if you have a physical or mental impairment that substantially limits a major life activity.

_____ **b.** If you have a disability, you must also be qualified to perform the essential functions or duties of a job, with or without reasonable accommodation. . . .

_____ **c.** An employer cannot require you to take a medical examination before you are offered a job.

_____ **d.** The part of the ADA enforced by the EEOC outlaws job discrimination by all employers, including state and local government employers, with 15 or more employees after July 26, 1994.

You would need to know the information in statements a, b, and d in order to know if you could file a charge with the EEOC. *Might* you have a basis to file a charge of discrimination with the EEOC? Why or why not?

_____

_____

Statement d tells you that you cannot file a charge. Even though you have a substantial disability and the skills and training for the job, the company has only 12 employees, so it does not have to follow the ADA.

 Tip   To apply information, be sure to consider all the relevant facts. Then evaluate your situation by applying each factor to your situation.

B. Practice

Read the case that follows. Then answer the questions.

You work for a manufacturing company with 45 employees. You work in customer service, but you have applied for a position as a sales representative. You are a good worker and get along well with customers on the telephone. You know you would do well in sales, and you heard your boss say you were the best candidate. But you are legally blind, and you sometimes need a little help getting around. You're afraid your boss won't promote you because customers might be uneasy when they see you. If you don't get the sales job, can you file a charge of discrimination with the EEOC?

1. Check each statement that would help you decide if you could file a charge of discrimination if you don't get the job.

   _____ **a.** Under the ADA, you have a disability if you have a physical or mental impairment that substantially limits a major life activity.

   _____ **b.** If you have a disability, you must also be qualified to perform the essential functions or duties of a job, with or without reasonable accommodation.

   _____ **c.** EEOC will encourage efforts of employers and individuals with disabilities to settle such differences through alternative methods of dispute resolution.

2. Do you think you may have a basis to file a charge of discrimination if you don't get the sales job? Explain.

   _____

   _____

3. Suppose you do get the job of sales representative. A hearing-impaired woman applies for your old job of customer service representative. The boss would like to hire her, except she needs an amplifier installed in the receiver to use a telephone. If she does not get the job, might she have a basis to file a charge of discrimination? Explain your answer.

   _____

   _____

▶ **Talk About It**
The brochure "The Americans with Disabilities Act" presents many details about the ADA that you or someone else might need to know. With a partner, make up a case in which a person with a disability may have been discriminated against in the workplace. Present the case to your classmates and have them try to decide if the person should contact the EEOC.

Write About It: Write a Fact Sheet

The brochure "The Americans with Disabilities Act" contains much information about the ADA. It's useful to be able to select the key facts from such a document. In this section, you will have a chance to write a fact sheet—a detailed list of important facts—based on information in the brochure. First study the sample, which shows how to write a fact sheet.

Study the Sample

Read the steps below to see what the writer considered as he developed his fact sheet.

Step 1: Picking a Topic. The writer decided to write a fact sheet of the information in the first four sections of the brochure on pages 61–62.

Step 2: Developing and Organizing the Fact Sheet. The writer listed the main points explained in each of the first four sections of the brochure. He used the headings to guide him. He wrote the topics in the form of questions and noted short answers to each question:

Who must obey the ADA?
> all employers with 15 or more employees after July 26, 1994

Who is protected by the ADA?
> people with disabilities who are qualified to work

What two requirements must a person meet?
> substantial impairment and qualified for the job

What is "reasonable accommodation"?
> change or adjustment that helps person with disability do job

What are the exceptions to reasonable accommodation?
> significant difficulty or expense

Now read his fact sheet on the next page. Then it will be your turn.

Your Turn

A. Prewriting

Step 1: Look at the information in the last four sections of the brochure, starting on page 63 with "Can an Employer Require Medical Examinations or Ask Questions About a Disability?"

Fact Sheet–Americans with Disabilities Act

Who must obey the ADA?

• All employers with 15 or more employees after July 26, 1994, must obey the ADA.

Who is protected by the ADA?

• Persons with a disability are protected.

What two requirements must be met?

1. You must have a substantial physical or mental impairment.
   • You have the disability now, you have a history of the disability, or the employer believes you have the disability.
   • The disability greatly limits a major life activity—like walking, talking, or hearing.
2. You must be qualified for the job.
   • You must have the required education, experience, skills, or licenses.
   • You must be able to do the job with or without "reasonable accommodation."

What is "reasonable accommodation"?

• Reasonable accommodation is any change or adjustment to a job or workplace that helps a person with a disability apply for or do a job or enjoy the same benefits as other workers.

What are the exceptions to reasonable accommodation?

An employer does not have to provide accommodation
• when the change is too costly for employer
• when the change is too difficult to make

Step 2: On separate paper, make a list of at least eight main points described in the last four sections of the brochure. Ask and answer questions, as the model on page 68 does.

B. Writing

On separate paper, use your list to write a fact sheet.

 Tip Being able to select the key facts from a document and write them in an outline is important for more than just creating fact sheets. You can also use this skill when reading important notices at work or studying school subjects.

▶ **Save your draft.** At the end of this unit, you will work with one of your drafts further.

Lesson 6 ▶ LEARNING GOALS

Strategy: Use your prior experience
Reading: Read a personal narrative
Skill: Recognize objective and subjective writing
Writing: Write a personal narrative

Before You Read

In "Subway Conductor," the author describes the special problems faced by women who took jobs with the New York City Transit Authority in the late 1970s. Before that time, motormen and conductors traditionally were men.

Think about women, such as female firefighters, who take jobs traditionally held by men. Think also of men, such as male nurses, who take jobs traditionally held by women.

1. Why might a person choose a job traditionally held by the opposite sex?

_____

_____

2. What might a person's co-workers think about working with this person?

_____

_____

3. What problems might both men and women face as they start working together?

_____

_____

Preview the Reading

From the title and the author's name, you learn that a woman is writing about being a subway conductor. Look at the illustrations for hints about the people and the workplace described in the selection.

Set Your Strategy: Use Your Prior Experience

Your **prior experience** is what you have learned from life so far. You can use your prior experience to help you understand what you read. Your prior experience with the workplace and your co-workers, with subways and trains, can add meaning to what the author tells you in "Subway Conductor." After you read the selection, you will have a chance to identify some prior experiences that helped you understand the story.

Beginning in the 1960s, federal laws were passed to ban job discrimination against women. Women began taking jobs that once were considered "men's work." What was it like for these women? "Subway Conductor" tells one woman's perspective.

Subway Conductor

Marian Swerdlow

In the late 1970s, the New York City Transit Authority opened the titles of motorman and conductor to female applicants. By the time I became a conductor in 1982, there were still very few women working in these titles. We remained oddities, pioneers.

Most people on the subway trains don't really have much of an idea what the motorman or the conductor does. The motorman works in the front of the train and drives it. The conductor works at or near the middle of the train, operates the doors and makes most of the announcements.

A lot of people think the subway conductor and motorman job must be easy or even fun to do. That wasn't my experience. The high noise level and the vibration are nerve-wracking. It's against the rules to use earplugs, though that never stopped me from protecting my hearing that way. The air is full of steel dust which gets in your eyes and your nose and gives your uniform a silvery sheen that the oldtimers call "silver dust." The trains are often brutally cold in the winter and hot as hell in the summer. The work is fairly dangerous: each employee averages one lost time accident a year and about one motorman or conductor out of a total six thousand dies in a work accident each year.

By the time you get off your train after a trip of around two hours, you are ready for a break. But usually you get less than ten minutes in the crew-room. At lunch, you might, if lucky, get thirty minutes. Even then, the crew room is pretty grim, dirty and noisy. Not exactly climate-controlled, either. The ones underground are the worst. The toilet facilities are unreliable, often smelly and sometimes flooded, and you can practically never get soap or towels. To make matters worse, most terminals do not have separate facilities for men and women, but more of that later.

All too quickly you are back "on the road." For a conductor, this is time to play "duck the rider." When I was working the Number 4 line, I was the target of an average of two attempted physical assaults a week. When I tell people this, they usually assume I must have done something to provoke my assailants—they just can't imagine that human beings would attack someone completely innocent. Well, guess again. The assaults were mostly from children! The conductor has to observe the train for three car lengths as it pulls out of each station. That means we have to have our heads out of the window of the cab as the train pulls out, until it moves 150 feet. The kids know this. They wait there on the platform getting ready to spit, hit or throw something as the conductor passes. They get a kick out of hitting someone who can't do anything back. Some of these kids look as young as seven or eight. Usually the injury is more psychological than physical, but not always.

As you can imagine, after eight hours of this, a conductor is dying to go home, unless he or she has a crying need for "soap," as overtime is called. But the average shift has been growing longer and it's now about nine hours. And, if anything goes wrong on the road, you can end up working many more hours without any choice or advance notice. So on my last return trip I'd always have my heart in my mouth, afraid of getting "turned," that is, being forced to make an extra trip.

Since the subways run seven days a week, and days off are picked according to seniority,[1] it takes at least five years for a conductor to get even part of the weekend off. Hours are also picked by seniority. My first year, I was forced to work evenings and nights. For motormen on some lines, it can take years to get onto days.

This is the job, whether you are male or female, but as women, especially "pioneers," we faced some extra problems.

1. **seniority** (seen/YOR/ih/tee) the position of having worked in a job longer than co-workers

There was only one other woman in my conductor's class, Helena. When we came out on the road we were bombarded with attention from our co-workers, who mostly wanted to know: "What does your husband think about you doing this?" This was a way of finding out whether we did have a lord-and-master, or were unattached. The first few months, I got propositioned so consistently that I finally joked about giving a civil service exam for the position, with a filing fee and a physical (which is what you have to do to become a conductor). I was relieved that no one took rejection personally—they were like someone who routinely looks in the coin return of pay phones to see if there's a quarter there, with the hope that you never know, you just might get lucky.

In some ways the men were happy to see us. We were a distraction, something different. But we were also a threat. Not to their jobs—the union and management had had a no layoff policy for years—but to their self-image. They saw themselves as doing a man's job. They had a big stake in believing they were doing a job only the superior sex could handle emotionally as well as physically. They really didn't believe that we could handle it, that we could have the presence of mind, the courage, the cool. But here we were.

Ironically, one of the results of their skepticism[2] was that, as individuals, we got a lot of praise. It really knocked their socks off when we handled a violent rider, or a door problem, or even just did our job competently. It didn't take much for a motorman to come into the crewroom telling all the others what a great conductor I was.

But even as each motorman or conductor thought his work partner was the glowing exception to general female helplessness, he was hungrily listening to, and repeating, tales which reinforced the old stereotypes.[3] Every time a

2. **skepticism** (SKEP/tih/SIH/zum) doubt
3. **stereotypes** (STEHR/ee/oh/TIPES) fixed ideas about an entire group

woman made a mistake it was endlessly repeated, and embroidered, and repeated, in crewrooms throughout the system.

Donna March was one of the first women to "go to the motors" (become a motorman). She was legendary for her knowledge of trains, her vulgar mouth and her sexual appetite. All of this made her particularly threatening to the men on the job.

Then one day she took the wrong "line-up" (track) heading for the wrong terminal. She tried to get back to the right track by backing up the train, which is absolutely forbidden, and she got caught. She was busted back to conductor. Now, plenty of men have backed up trains, and plenty of men have been caught and busted. It gets discussed in their terminal a few days and then it is dropped. But when Donna screwed up, it was talked about all over the IRT for years. After Donna got her handles back (was restored to motorman) the guys in the crewroom started talking about it all over again!

When I first came out to the road, I was assigned to midnights. My very first night on the road, I was sent out of my usual line, to the Number 1 line. On my second trip, two of the riders

shot each other right outside of my cab. That kind of thing never happened again on my train, but it happened my first night when I was brand new. Well, I was not delighted, but I never thought of quitting. The next night I was back on my usual Number 4 line. About a year later, I worked on the 1 again and all the guys said to me: "What are you doing here? You quit when you had the shooting!" That was their image of women: the job was too rough, what we'd see would be too much for our maidenly delicacy. That image was much more convenient than the facts.

But as more and more of us came on, did the job, didn't scream and faint when the riders shot each other, when the cabs blew up (as mine did once), when people fell between the cars, or when riders threatened us with mayhem, it became obvious that, yes, we really could do the job.

The men never stopped believing that we were given extra privileges—privileges they as men did not receive. For example, they believed "all the women conductors go down to Jay Street." Jay Street is the Transit Authority headquarters in Brooklyn. There are a few clerical positions there reserved for conductors. It *is* possible that a lot of the first women to get called for conductor ended up there, which might have had as much to do with the Transit Authority not wanting women on the road as with what the women themselves wanted. But as far as some of our male co-workers were concerned, that's where all the women went— straight to those cushy desk jobs, while they slaved on the road. A friend of mine once met a conductor at a bar, who gave her a song-and-dance about the women all going to Jay Street. My friend quickly referred to me as evidence against this. "Oh sure," he responded, "I know Marian. Tell her Redford says hi." Almost immediately after that I had to visit headquarters for some reason, probably unpleasant, and who do I find there, working a cushy desk job, but Conductor Redford.

Another legend had it that women never worked terminals or hours they did not want. I sure didn't know that when I spent six months working nights on the 2 line, which was nicknamed "the Beast." Helena didn't know that when she got stuck working with the farebox on the 5 line. The box weighs at least thirty-five pounds and she, just like the men, had to carry it on and off the trains, and up and down steps, several times in an evening. One night, lifting it, Helena felt a sharp twinge. She'd gotten a hernia. She was out for a total of almost two years. The Transit Authority disputed her worker's comp claim, too, ludicrously[4] claiming that she came on the job with the hernia. That's the special way the Transit Authority treated women.

There was also the tale that the signal system was changed to accommodate women motormen. In the early 1980s, some signals were changed to make it easier to bypass them if they mal-functioned. The old way, the motorman had to fasten down a heavy trip arm next to the tracks; the new way, he or she could just insert a key in the signal. Well, the guys all said it was because women weren't strong enough to fasten down the trip arm. The change might have had more to do with a fatality in the summer of 1980. A motorman was killed when he accidentally touched the third rail while fastening down a trip arm (the third rail carries 600 volts of direct current). And he wasn't a woman.

Management's main policy towards the women on the job could be summed up as "malign[5] neglect." They refused to recognize we'd arrived. We wore uniforms designed for men, which meant they fit terribly. They felt awful and looked worse. More problematic was the absence of separate toilet facilities for women and men at most terminals.

The trouble of sharing with our male co-workers was exacerbated when the toilet cubicles lacked latches and sometimes even doors. Outside the cubicles were the urinals, which meant that even when locks were put on the cubicles, it wouldn't necessarily spare you and your male co-worker an embarrassing encounter as you stepped out of your cubicle.

The big Transit Authority innovation was to put latches on the doors of the restroom itself. But this meant that one solitary woman in the restroom, if she locked the restroom door to keep men from using the urinals and risking that oh-so-embarrassing encounter, could effectively prevent anyone else in the terminal, male or female, from entering to urinate, wash their hands, or get water for the kettle. With lunches and breaks inhumanly short, this created tensions between the men and the women. When I started a petition for a separate women's toilet at the Number 4 line terminal, Woodlawn, there wasn't a man who wouldn't sign it. The sheets I posted on the walls quickly filled up with signatures. Unfortunately, management was much less cooperative than our male co-workers.

One of the times I faced disciplinary charges arose out of the unisex toilet situation. About a year after I came on the job, I one day ate or drank something that did not agree with me. I was working out of a terminal in which there was no lock on the restroom, and no doors on the toilet cubicles. I just could not bring myself to use the toilet.

I tried to book[6] sick. I was told I could either go to a hospital or face immediate suspension. I decided to continue working. I fainted at Times Square at the height of the rush hour. After I revived, I had to talk to the bigshot at headquarters, the desk trainmaster, for this infraction[7] of passing out. He wasn't satisfied when I explained what had made me sick and told me that I faced disciplinary charges. I said: "I think this is the Transit Authority's fault for not having separate facilities for women." He said: "Next you'll want powder rooms." This guy is now the chief of the subway command center.

---

4. **ludicrously** (LOO/duh/krus/lee) absurdly; ridiculously
5. **malign** (muh/LINE) evil; injurious

6. **book** write or register in a book or list
7. **infraction** (in/FRAK/shun) a breaking of a rule or law

The union presides over all this misery. Local 100 of the Transport Workers Union (AFL-CIO) has been so unresponsive that most motormen and conductors see it as a company union. No copy of any contract was available to the members the whole time I worked as a conductor. (One was given out in late 1987, after a ten-year wait.) There are no elected shop stewards, and there was no shop steward training from 1981 to 1986. Union officers blame their own members for the worsening conditions of work, tell the membership, "You're lucky to have jobs," and generally justify management policies.

The union officers were pretty much indifferent to whatever special problems we faced as women. One such issue was maternity leave. Boda Trinshaw was probably the first female operative to become pregnant. When I tried to get information from the union regarding maternity leave I was given an elaborate runaround, probably because no one knew, and no one wanted to take the trouble to find out, our rights. One union officer I spoke with angrily accused Boda of "stirring up" all the women operatives. Another officer confided in me that his brother officers' attitude was basically, "Why didn't she keep her legs together?" This comment was made even though her husband was also a conductor and a union member.

I was very interested in being active in rank-and-file[8] efforts to democratize and revitalize the local. At the beginning, I tried to work with the experienced union dissidents[9] who had been influential in the late seventies. Their strength culminated in the 1980 New York transit strike, which was won on the picket line by the workers and lost at the bargaining table by union leaders who wanted to discourage future militance.

The "old" dissidents were not much better than the union leaders in many ways, including their

---

8. **rank-and-file** ordinary members of a group, not the leaders
9. **dissidents** (DIH/suh/dents) people who disagree with the way things are

attitudes towards women. They were suspicious of the early attempt of women on the job to organize the "Lady Motormen's Association" (bad name, good idea). And in the summer of 1984, the old dissidents tried to exclude Donna March from their slate for convention delegate because of what they considered her reputation for promiscuity!

I was very fortunate, though, because I found other rank-and-filers I could work with, who generally had better attitudes about women and women's issues, on and off the job. We founded a rank-and-file newsletter, *Hell on Wheels*. Working on that rag was by far the best part of the transit job for me.

The four years I worked as a conductor, more and more women came on the job. Almost all of them were black. Women enter this field because, compared to the jobs in the pink-collar[10] ghetto, transit offers better pay, better benefits and better opportunities for promotion. Working as a conductor is difficult for women because of the intense contact with the public, though it's hard to

---

10. **pink-collar** describing jobs usually held by women

know whether women get more physical or verbal abuse than men.

Motors is a step up from conductor and gets you away from the public. But it also requires strength and more physical confidence than I, for one, had. A motorman can expect to spend a lot of time on the tracks, both in the hole (the tunnels) and on the structure (the elevated tracks). I was, to be quite honest, afraid of this work. Afraid of the third rail, the "shoes" protruding from the train which were also electrified, the trains speeding by, and, on the structure, the huge gaps between the ties you had to jump across. I didn't feel I could refuse an order, no matter how dangerous I thought it was, because it would just fuel the crewroom scuttlebutt that women couldn't do the job. And if, god forbid, I were clumsy or unlucky enough to get myself badly hurt, it would cast doubts on any woman's ability to do the job and survive. So I stayed in my conductor blues (this refers to the uniform, but for me it got to be a state of mind). But plenty of women went to motors, plenty more are going, and my hat's off to them.

I left transit in the summer of 1986. Today, there are many more women operating on the subways than when I came on. They are no longer oddities, no longer pioneers. But working conditions are still worsening for transit workers, and the special problems faced by women in these jobs are still not recognized.

▶ **Revisit Your Strategy: Use Your Prior Experience**
Which of the following experiences did you know something about before you read the narrative? Check each one.

_____ Starting a new job	_____ Writing a newsletter
_____ Being the only male or female on the job	_____ Working under poor conditions
	_____ Being a victim of prejudice
_____ Riding a subway train	_____ Being misunderstood
_____ Being a conductor	_____ Being sexually harassed
_____ Being a motorman	_____ Being a victim of false rumors
_____ Fighting for your rights	_____ Getting along with co-workers
_____ Finding solutions to problems	_____ Dealing with management

You checked the experiences you already knew about. Did thinking about your own experiences help you relate to the people in the narrative?

After You Read

A. Comprehension Check

1. A subway conductor on the road can expect to experience each of the following *except*
   - (1) high noise levels
   - (3) weekends off
   - (2) physical assaults
   - (4) dust and grit

2. One of the extra problems faced by the female "pioneers" in the transit system was
   - (1) being granted special privileges
   - (2) being stereotyped as helpless females
   - (3) taking the civil service exam
   - (4) paying high union dues

3. Which of the following is one reason women sought work with the transit authority?
   - (1) the working conditions
   - (2) the intense contact with the public
   - (3) the high status of the jobs
   - (4) the opportunity for promotion

4. Men in the transit system felt threatened by their female co-workers because women
   - (1) were getting men fired
   - (2) received more praise than men did
   - (3) distracted the men
   - (4) proved that they could handle the job

5. In the transit system, women
   - (1) get promoted more often than men
   - (2) make better salaries than men
   - (3) have special problems men don't face
   - (4) have more fun than the men have

6. In the phrase "as more and more of us came on, did the job, didn't scream and faint when . . . riders threatened us with *mayhem*," *mayhem* means
   - (1) damage or violence
   - (3) weapons
   - (2) robbery
   - (4) stopping the train

B. Read between the Lines

Check each statement that you think Marian Swerdlow would agree with. Find evidence in the selection to support your choices.

_____ 1. Women take jobs traditionally held by men to earn higher pay.

_____ 2. Women who work in men's jobs are out to prove they are better than men.

_____ 3. Men's ideas about what women can and cannot do are generally wrong.

_____ 4. Women who work in jobs traditionally held by men deserve special privileges.

_____ 5. Women who take jobs traditionally held by men have more to prove than men do.

C. Think beyond the Reading

Discuss these questions with a partner. Answer them in writing on separate paper if you wish.

1. What does the author mean when she states that her conductor blues became a state of mind? Do you think she had reason to feel that way? Explain.

2. Look back at your answers to Before You Read on page 70. Compare and contrast them with what you read in the selection "Subway Conductor."

Think About It: Recognize Objective and Subjective Writing

In **objective writing,** the writer tries to present facts without being influenced by personal feelings or beliefs. **Subjective writing,** on the other hand, includes the writer's opinions, interpretations, emotions, values, and prejudices.

The reading in Lesson 5, the brochure "The Americans with Disabilities Act," is a good example of objective writing. It presents facts about the act, not feelings about it. When people write about their own experiences, as Marian Swerdlow did in "Subway Conductor," some of that writing is going to be subjective.

It is important to be able to recognize subjective writing. Like Swerdlow, an author writing subjectively may simply be describing personal reactions to experiences. But an author may also write subjectively to influence or persuade you—and often such authors include carefully selected facts and try to *sound* objective.

A. Look at Objective and Subjective Writing

Each of the following excerpts from "Subway Conductor" contains both objective (expressing facts) and subjective (expressing thoughts and feelings) phrases. Read each one, and circle the objective phrases. Underline the subjective phrases.

1. "The high noise level and vibration are nerve-wracking."

2. "The trains are . . . brutally cold in winter. . . ."

3. ". . . and hot as hell in summer."

4. "After a trip of about two hours, you are ready for a break."

5. ". . . the crew room is pretty grim, dirty and noisy."

6. "To make matters worse, most terminals do not have separate facilities for men and women."

You should have circled "high noise level and vibration," "cold in winter," "hot . . . in summer," "a trip of about two hours," "dirty and noisy," and "most terminals do not have separate facilities for men and women." These phrases are objective—they give facts about the transit system. You should have underlined "nerve-wracking," "brutally," "as hell," "you are ready for a break," "pretty grim," and "To make matters worse." These phrases are subjective—they describe the author's reactions to her experiences.

 Tip   When you read, ask yourself what the author's purpose was. Watch for subjective writing, including carefully selected facts, being used to sway you in favor of the author's beliefs or opinions. Decide if you really agree with the author's ideas.

B. Practice

Reread these excerpts from "Subway Conductor." Underline subjective language the author uses to express thoughts and feelings.

1. ▶ But even as each motorman or conductor thought his work partner was the glowing exception to general female helplessness, he was hungrily listening to, and repeating, tales which reinforced the old stereotypes. Every time a woman made a mistake it was endlessly repeated, and embroidered, and repeated, in crewrooms throughout the system.

2. ▶ Management's main policy towards the women on the job could be summed up as "malign neglect." They refused to recognize we'd arrived. We wore uniforms designed for men, which meant they fit terribly. They felt awful and looked worse.

3. ▶ The union presides over all this misery. Local 100 of the Transport Workers Union (AFL-CIO) has been so unresponsive that most motormen and conductors see it as a company union. . . .

   . . .The union officers were pretty much indifferent to whatever special problems we faced as women. One such issue was maternity leave. Boda Trinshaw was probably the first female operative to become pregnant. When I tried to get information from the union regarding maternity leave I was given an elaborate runaround, probably because no one knew, and no one wanted to take the trouble to find out, our rights.

4. Rewrite excerpt 2 on separate paper, deleting the subjective language or replacing it with objective language. Then share your objective version with a partner or your instructor.

> ▶ **Talk About It**
> The first-person narrator of "Subway Conductor" reports only what *she* saw and felt. She doesn't know the thoughts of the other people involved. Discuss and list some concerns that the men may have had about working alongside women. If you like, role-play a discussion among a group of the men complaining about working with women.

Write About It: Write a Personal Narrative

A personal narrative tells about something that happened to the writer. For example, Marian Swerdlow writes about what happened to her as one of the first women conductors of the New York Transit Authority. As you did in Lesson 4, you will have a chance to write a personal narrative about something that happened to you. First study the sample, which shows how to write a personal narrative.

Study the Sample

Read the steps below to see what the writer considered as he developed his narrative.

Step 1: Picking a Topic. The writer of the narrative below decided to write about his experience as an African American department store Santa. He wrote this working title: "Being an African American Santa."

Tip Giving the first draft a working title—a title that simply tells the topic—can help guide your writing. Once you have finished your draft, you can revise the title so that it also catches the reader's interest.

Step 2: Developing and Organizing the Narrative. The writer started with the event that happened first, adding details that described the action. Then he listed the other events and details in the order they happened.

> **First:** I enrolled in Santa Claus training program.
>   **Detail:** I was the only African American participant.
>   **Detail:** Most of the others didn't think I should be there.
>   **Detail:** I learned to be the best Santa I could be.

↓

> **Second:** I got a job in a department store.
>   **Detail:** I started out nervous, but then relaxed and played the role.
>   **Detail:** The first little girl believed I was Santa.
>   **Detail:** The white children didn't seem bothered that I was black.
>   **Detail:** Some white parents asked when the "real" Santa would be back.

↓

> **Third:** The experience turned out to be very positive.
>   **Detail:** All the children made it worthwhile.
>   **Detail:** The black children made it especially rewarding.

Now read the writer's personal narrative on the next page. Then it will be your turn.

Here Comes Santa Claus

One autumn in the early 1970s, I enrolled in a Santa Claus training program. Some of my classmates weren't so jolly when they saw me. Let's just say that their laughs were less than hearty and their eyes glared more than twinkled. You see, I am African American, and it was clear that most of my white classmates believed Santa Claus should be white. I knew I wouldn't change their prejudices, so I didn't try. All I wanted was to learn to be the best Santa possible—from the ho-ho-ho to the pillow-soft belly—and that's what I did.

My friends warned me I'd never get a job, but I did—in a small neighborhood department store. When that first child approached me, I was a little nervous. But I took a deep breath, smiled with my eyes (the white beard all but covered my mouth), and said, "Come on and tell old Santa what you want for Christmas." The little blond girl eagerly climbed onto my lap and asked me how my reindeer were. It turned out that none of the white children seemed bothered by my color. All they saw was Santa Claus. On the other hand, some white parents rudely asked what time the "real" Santa would be back from his break.

I managed to keep a twinkle in my eye, though, because the children made it so worthwhile. It was especially rewarding when black children came to me. I could tell the second it registered that I was black. Their eyes would light up brightly, and they would get so excited. They had finally met a Santa Claus they could completely identify with.

Your Turn

A. Prewriting

Step 1: Choose a topic from the list below or one of your own. Write about a time when you

- did something that someone of your gender, age, or race didn't traditionally do
- tried to fit in at a new job
- handled a dangerous situation
- fought for your rights
- were one of the first to do something
- solved a long-standing problem

Step 2: List the events and details in the order they happened on separate paper. Notice which details are objective and which are subjective.

B. Writing

Now write your personal narrative on separate paper. Give it a catchy title.

▶ **Save your draft.** At the end of this unit, you will work with one of your drafts further.

Writing Skills Mini-Lesson: Pronoun Agreement

A pronoun is a word that takes the place of a noun. A pronoun must agree with its **antecedent**—the noun that it stands for—three ways: in case, number, and gender.

Antecedent   **Pronoun**

Anita was confined to a wheelchair, but **she** wanted a job.

Case is determined by how the word is used in a sentence. There are three cases:
- **Nominative** for subjects: *I, you, he, she, it, we, you,* and *they.*
- **Objective** for objects of verbs and prepositions: *me, you, him, her, it, us, you,* and *them.*
- **Possessive** to show ownership: *my, mine, your, yours, his, her, hers, its, our, ours, your, yours, their, theirs.*

Number means singular *(I, you, he, she,* and *it)* or plural *(we, you,* and *they).*

Gender means male or female *(he, him, his* or *she, her, hers).*

Follow these rules about pronouns and their antecedents.

1. **Be sure the pronoun has a clear antecedent.** If it is not clear, rewrite the sentence.

   Unclear: Anita talked with her sister about what she could do.
   (About what who could do, Anita or her sister?)
   Clear: **Anita's** sister gave **her** advice about looking for work.

2. **Be sure the pronoun agrees with its antecedent in case, number, and gender.**

   Wrong: **Her** and her sister made a list of jobs Anita could do.
   Right: **She** and her sister made a list of jobs Anita could do.

   Wrong: Each woman tried **their** best to think of all possibilities.
   Right: Each woman tried **her** best to think of all possibilities.

   Wrong: Anita asked one of her friends if **they** would help too.
   Right: Anita asked one of her friends if **she** (or **he**) would help too.

Practice: On separate paper, rewrite the paragraph, using pronouns correctly. There may be more than one way to fix some sentences.

> To help in her job search, each of Anita's friends shared their ideas about job hunting with her. Then her and her friends made a list of places with job openings. I met Anita when her and a friend came to my office to apply for a job. After her and I had talked for a while, I knew she would be a good receptionist. While she filled out an application, I talked with my boss. Him and I discussed her qualifications and agreed Anita's wheelchair would not be a problem. Then him and me offered Anita the receptionist's job. She was so excited she thanked the boss and I over and over. And she has been a big help to he and I ever since.

Reading Review

Bithiah Carter

Donna Ballard

Changing Perceptions

It's 6:30 A.M.—A subway platform is full of people waiting for a Manhattan-bound train, which has been delayed by a water main break two stations away. Bithiah Carter, thirty-one, stands at the edge of the platform, leans forward, and looks for the two headlights that should have appeared in the dark tunnel fifteen minutes ago. A few minutes pass and the train pulls into the station. A frustrated mob pushes its way into the double doors and pensively waits for the conductor's admonition to "Step in. Stand clear of the door." Compressed back to back with other commuters, the young businesswoman holds on tightly to the strap hanger for the next six stops into Manhattan while reading a quarter-folded paper. She has a few minutes to find out what didn't make news on Bloomberg, a financial news retrieval service.

Day after day, for eight years, this has been the morning ritual for Bithiah Carter, thirty-one, salesperson at W. R. Lazard, a minority-owned investment bank based in New York. For many career women, the motivation to be in highly competitive careers such as sales—careers that require a large degree of persistence—is to be paid well and recognized in their profession. However, for some women, there are other reasons. Bithiah Carter, an energetic and attractive woman, has another reason, which she shares with me at her home in Brooklyn. Inside a modestly decorated apartment, Bithiah explains over a glass of wine that one of the other reasons she is motivated to be in her career is to change perceptions. The Cleveland State graduate from Ohio stated, "I am pushed to be in a business career first and foremost because of the knowledge I acquire. That may sound a little clichéd,[1] but that really is my reason." Bithiah explains further, "Like anyone who works, of course there are the basic needs that we must meet. Those needs drive us to get up each morning and go in. But whatever underlying reason we chose certain areas versus others has more to do with the way we see ourselves and the way in which we want others to see us. For example, it amazes me that some of us have limited views on what we can do in the business world. There have been a number of times where others are shocked when I tell them what I do for a living. That tells me a lot about how we, specifically, as African-Americans, still today, perceive what we are capable of doing. And I'll admit, sometimes it bothers me." But Bithiah is not trying to alter everyone's perception of what she is capable of doing professionally. "No, I don't try to change the perception of every person I meet. However, I do hope I am making a difference with younger people—the children," she says. As a visiting mentor to a class of third graders at a local elementary school in her community, she says,

1. clichéd (klee/SHADE) overused, trite, stale

"That's where I hope to change the mindset. It's exciting to watch the faces of children brighten with interest when they learn I am doing something that is different from what they have been taught or exposed to. It piques[2] their curiosity and makes them want to learn more. Of course, I don't expect all of them to want to grow up and become brokers or salespeople. But I do hope their expectations of what they are capable of accomplishing, in spite of everything around them, has been changed."

"Also," she says, switching to a lighter tone, "I am motivated to be in this business because I want to know everything.

"Call me nosey! I've always been the kind of person who wanted to know what's happening in the world, the business world. Why did this company sell its interest in this company? Or why will one company decide to move its headquarters to another country and what will that mean for people with jobs at that company?

"I don't care whether you're buying toothpaste or a new car. Every dollar you spend translates at some point in time to buy or sell for investors. And that drives business. Realizing all of this is at the heart of what drives me to be a business professional.

"Often someone will ask me how do I handle working in an environment made up of mostly white males or do I feel I can really get ahead when there are so few black women in senior positions? I always find those questions interesting, but my answer is usually simple. I tell them, 'How does this environment differ from many other places in America or corporate America?' How about finding success? Success?" she says, thinking deeply about the definition. "Well, for the first time in history, we are reaching heights that we have never reached before. No longer are we only in the back offices, but some of us have moved into the boardrooms. You see us at some of the top levels in corporations and even running our own businesses. But that doesn't define how successful we have become as professional black women. I think our success is better defined by how we take what we have gained from our experiences, personally and professionally, and use it to advance our presence in the next century. In my mind, that's making sure the generation to follow can benefit from our success and mistakes."

---

2. **piques** (peeks) arouses

Choose the best answer to each question.

1. Bithiah Carter can be characterized by all of the following *except*
   (1) highly motivated (3) competent
   (2) self-confident (4) selfish

2. From reading the article, you can infer that the author
   (1) didn't like Bithiah Carter
   (2) was prejudiced against career women
   (3) admired Bithiah Carter
   (4) was completely subjective in her writing

3. One way that Bithiah Carter is similar to Marian Swerdlow is
   (1) they are both in danger of being injured on the job
   (2) they are both women in traditionally male jobs
   (3) they are both in highly paid professions
   (4) their jobs are physically demanding

4. One way that Bithiah Carter is different from Humphrey Boone is
   (1) she is a well-paid banker
   (2) she faces prejudice regularly
   (3) she works for a minority-owned bank
   (4) she is successful in her job

Facts About
National Origin Discrimination

U.S. Equal Opportunity Commission

Title VII of the Civil Rights Act of 1964 protects individuals against employment discrimination on the basis of national origin as well as race, color, religion and sex.

It is unlawful to discriminate against any employee or applicant because of the individual's national origin. No one can be denied equal employment opportunity because of birthplace, ancestry, culture, or linguistic characteristics common to a specific ethnic group. Equal employment opportunity cannot be denied because of

- marriage or association with persons of a national origin group;
- membership or association with specific ethnic promotion groups;
- attendance or participation in schools, churches, temples or mosques generally associated with a national origin group; or
- a surname associated with a national origin group.

Speak-English-Only Rule

A rule requiring employees to speak only English at all times on the job may violate Title VII, unless an employer shows it is necessary for conducting business. If an employer believes the English-only rule is critical for business purposes, employees have to be told when they must speak English and the consequences for violating the rule. Any negative employment decision based on breaking the English-only rule will be considered evidence of discrimination if the employer did not tell employees of the rule.

Accent

An employer must show a legitimate nondiscriminatory reason for the denial of employment opportunity because of an individual's accent or manner of speaking. Investigations will focus on the qualifications of the person and whether his or her accent or manner of speaking had a detrimental effect on job performance. Requiring employees or applicants to be fluent in English may violate Title VII if the rule is adopted to exclude individuals of a particular national origin and is not related to job performance.

Harassment

Harassment on the basis of national origin is a violation of Title VII. An ethnic slur or other verbal or physical conduct because of an individual's nationality are harassment if they

- create an intimidating, hostile or offensive working environment;
- unreasonably interfere with work performance; or
- negatively affect an individual's employment opportunities.

Employers have a responsibility to maintain a workplace free of national origin harassment. Employers may be responsible for any on-the-job harassment by their agents and supervisory employees, regardless of whether the acts were authorized or specifically forbidden by the employer. Under certain circumstances, an employer may be responsible for the acts of non-employees who harass their employees at work.

Immigration-Related Practices Which May Be Discriminatory

The Immigration Reform and Control Act of 1986 (IRCA) requires employers to prove all employees hired after November 6, 1986, are legally authorized to work in the United States.

IRCA also prohibits discrimination based on national origin or citizenship. An employer who singles out individuals of a particular national origin or individuals who appear to be foreign to provide employment verification may have violated both IRCA and Title VII. Employers who impose citizenship requirements or give preference to U.S. citizens in hiring or employment opportunities may have violated IRCA, unless these are legal or contractual requirements for particular jobs. Employers also may have violated Title VII if a requirement or preference has the purpose or effect of discriminating against individuals of a particular national origin.

Choose the best answer to each question.

5. According to the IRCA, from whom must an employer request proof that they can legally work in this country?
   (1) no one
   (2) only those who look foreign
   (3) only immigrants
   (4) all workers

6. Which of the following persons is protected from job discrimination by Title VII?
   (1) a man who has lived in the U.S. for five years and came *without* legal permission
   (2) a woman who is disabled yet qualified for the job
   (3) a man who cannot speak any English
   (4) a woman whose grandparents immigrated to the United States from Iran

7. An employer may be in violation of Title VII if
   (1) one employee personally dislikes another employee
   (2) an employee tells ethnic jokes in the lunchroom
   (3) the employer hired an applicant because she could speak both Spanish and English
   (4) the employer did not hire a foreign-born applicant because he lacked the experience of other applicants

8. Because the selection is written from an objective point of view, it
   (1) describes feelings
   (2) arouses emotions
   (3) states factual information
   (4) expresses personal thoughts

The Writing Process

In Unit 2, you wrote three first drafts. Choose the piece that you would like to work with further. You will revise, edit, and make a final copy of this draft.
   _____ your personal narrative about a time you were an outsider on page 58
   _____ your fact sheet on page 68
   _____ your narrative about something that happened to you on page 80

Find the first draft you chose. Then turn to page 176 in this book. Follow steps 3, 4, and 5 in the Writing Process to create a final draft.

As you revise, check your draft to be sure of the following:

Personal narrative: You include how successful or unsuccessful you were in being accepted.

Fact sheet: The fact sheet includes an explanation of each main point covered in the brochure.

Personal narrative: You express your thoughts and feelings about your experience and include a good title.

Unit 3 Resolving Conflict

All of us disagree with family members and friends at times. We may have conflicts with our boss or co-workers. We may be bothered by a rude customer or annoyed by loud neighbors. Resolving, or settling, a conflict is often not easy. But unless we learn to handle conflicts, we may risk our jobs and our relationships with people.

In this unit, you will read about some ways to resolve problems with neighbors. You will read advice on how to calm complaining customers. And you will read a story about a young man who learned a valuable lesson about conflict.

Before you begin Unit 3, think about a conflict you had to resolve recently. What did you learn from the experience?

▶ **Be an Active Reader**

As you read the selections in this unit
- Put a question mark (?) by things you do not understand.
- <u>Underline</u> words you do not know. Try to use context clues to figure them out.

After you read each selection in this unit
- Reread sections you marked with a question mark. If they still do not make sense, discuss them with a partner or your instructor.
- Look at words you <u>underlined</u>. Discuss any words you still don't understand with a partner or your instructor, or look them up in a dictionary.

Lesson 7

LEARNING GOALS

Strategy: Use your prior experience
Reading: Read a magazine article
Skill: Analyze problems and solutions
Writing: Write a problem/solution essay

Before You Read

The magazine article "The Neighbors from Hell" describes disputes among neighbors that were not easily resolved. It also offers suggestions for dealing with problem neighbors. Before you read the article, think about the experiences you have had with your own neighbors. Then answer the following questions.

1. What types of things might neighbors argue about?

_____

2. What is one thing you should do to resolve differences with a neighbor?

_____

3. What is one thing you should *not* do to resolve differences with a neighbor?

_____

4. Why do you think people sometimes do unreasonable things in neighbor disputes?

_____

Preview the Reading

Read the title, the first paragraph, and the headings to get an idea of what the article is about. Look at the illustration for other clues about the article.

Set Your Strategy: Use Your Prior Experience

You can use your **prior experience,** what you have learned from life, to help you understand this article, "The Neighbors from Hell." As you read the article, think about your own experiences with neighbors. When you are finished reading the article, you will have a chance to identify the experiences that helped you understand the selection.

Neighbors may live in the apartment upstairs, in the house
next door, or two miles down a country road. What happens when a neighbor
creates a problem? Read to find out how some neighbors tried
to solve their problems and what they might have done differently.

The Neighbors from Hell

Mark Stuart Gill

Their kids are loud and unruly, their dog barks all night and their house is an eyesore. If you complain, it only makes matters worse. But there is hope for this all-too-common problem.

The fifteen-year feud between the Drinkward family of Redondo Beach, California and the man next door started with an absurdly small incident.

One day, the Drinkwards say, their teenage son was washing their car, and some soapy water ran onto the neighbor's lawn. An argument erupted. The next day, they recall, the neighbor, a man in his seventies, painted a white line down the middle of the driveway and forbade the Drinkwards to cross it. (The neighbor declined to be interviewed for this story.) "I thought it was ridiculous," says Ann Drinkward. "I told my family to stay on our side of the line and the problem would go away."

But it didn't. When leaves from the Drinkwards' juniper trees fell into the neighbor's yard, Ann says, he'd dump them back on her property. And, when the Drinkwards built an addition onto their house, the neighbor reported them to the city for possible violation of building permits. "My husband had all the permits," says Ann. "He's a building inspector, for goodness sake!"

Finally, two years ago, says Ann, when communication from next door came only through registered mail, she'd had enough. In an effort to be friendly, she'd drop by with some fresh-baked cookies or a loaf of bread and chat with the neighbor.

For a few months, all was well. But then, according to Ann, the neighbor revived the feud, threatening the Drinkwards with a lawsuit for property damage. The reason? Roots from the juniper trees had crossed onto his property.

Under Siege

Across the country, these types of neighbor nightmares are becoming commonplace. The American Bar Association estimates that neighborhood disputes now account for up to 45 percent of misdemeanor[1] charges filed in U.S. courts each year. The complaints fall into three leading categories: vandalism from children and pets, boundary trees (for instance, a neighbor's maple blocking your view) and excessive noise. Other common charges stem from automobile parking, obnoxious odors and "spite" fences, legal terminology for high or ugly fences built specifically to annoy a neighbor.

As trivial[2] as these irritations may seem, when they occur over and over they can spark all-out war. For instance, in Texas, after two boys damaged a neighbor's shrubs while playing ball, the neighbor tried to run them down with a car. In one California town, a man was so enraged by persistent barking from his neighbor's dog that he taped shut the pet's mouth. The dog died, and the man now faces criminal charges for animal cruelty. In a Connecticut neighborhood, when a family

1. **misdemeanor** (mis/di/MEE/ner) a minor crime
2. **trivial** (TRIH/vee/ul) not important; small

refused to trim their messy weeping-willow tree, someone drilled holes in the tree's trunk and poisoned it.

What is it about neighbor disputes that sets otherwise rational people at each other's throats? The whole issue of home and neighborhood is emotionally charged, experts say. "Your house is supposed to be a haven from a hectic world, the place you can be king of your castle," says Cora Jordan, an attorney in Oxford, Mississippi, and author of *Neighbor Law* (Nolo Press).

And because of our neighbors' sheer proximity, we tend to react to them as extended family, according to Bob Hauer, a personal-injury lawyer who handles neighbor disputes in Minneapolis. "You never have a simple legal problem with an annoying neighbor," he says. "It's a lifestyle problem, a psychological problem. You start fighting with the folks next door, and it's like a marriage gone bad—except you can't divorce them."

When a neighbor problem arises, a person's first impulse is usually avoidance. "Either you can't risk insulting or offending them by bringing up a problem, or you feel helpless, like there is no feasible[3] solution," says Arthur T. Toole, of the Institute for Mediation[4] and Conflict Resolution, Inc., in New York City. "So you do nothing."

And lawsuits are also usually a poor solution. "Lawsuits often just mask or neutralize the

---

3. **feasible** (FEE/zuh/bul) possible; reasonable
4. **mediation** (MEE/dee/AY/shun) a way to settle a dispute in which a third person helps the two sides come to terms

immediate problem, creating even larger power struggles," warns Mark Warda, an attorney in Clearwater, Florida, and author of *Neighbor vs. Neighbor: Legal Rights Of Neighbors In Dispute* (Sphinx Publishing, 1991). "Courts hate neighbor lawsuits because the neighbors find something else to fight about."

What You Can Do

Experts say the most effective and satisfying way to solve neighbor disputes is to handle them yourself.

To begin with, be aware of your rights. When a neighbor does something so unreasonable that it constitutes a wrongful act or injury, he or she has broken "a nuisance law." These laws vary from community to community, but they are often very detailed. For instance, in Farmington, New Mexico, music played on private property is not allowed to exceed fifty decibels at night.

Check your local laws at the town clerk's office or the public library. If you have legal grounds to complain, show your neighbor a copy of the ordinance.[5]

Unfortunately, being on the right side of the law isn't always enough. To prevent the situation from turning into a battle, keep in mind that different types of neighbor problems call for different strategies:

Noise Thirty-seven-year-old Barbara Solomon,[*] of San Francisco, owns a vacation home in Seattle, where her family "escapes for peace and quiet." But a year ago, her next-door neighbor leased his house to four men in their twenties who were in a rock band. Every night, Barbara and her husband were levitated out of their bed by the screech of guitars.

"When I complained," she recalls, "they just looked at me and said, 'Noise? This is important music.' "

This reaction is very common, according to Dan Joyce, executive director of the Cleveland

---

5. **ordinance** (ORD/nunss) a local law
*Name has been changed.

Mediation Center. "Don't assume your neighbor realizes he or she is even creating a nuisance," he says.

Also, remember that noise is subjective. "Judging or interpreting the other person's behavior only alienates[6] them," says Debra Bass, communications vice president of the Community Associations Institute, an organization that represents condo and homeowner associations outside Washington, D.C. Instead, "give information about your own situation and feelings."

That's what Barbara did. When she explained that the band was keeping her family awake at night, they agreed to play only during the day with the windows closed. But eventually, the late-night jam sessions started up again.

At that point, Barbara presented the owner of the house next door with a petition signed by eight other neighbors. Within a month, the band moved out.

Kids and pets Children and domestic animals have the greatest potential to tear a neighborhood apart. Take the case of Michael Rubin, a civil trial lawyer in North Hollywood, California, who has been embroiled in one of the most bitter neighbor lawsuits in the nation for the last few years.

In 1989, Rubin's neighbors, the Schilds, erected a basketball hoop for their son about thirty feet from Rubin's bedroom window. One day, "I was so exhausted from work, I had to take a nap," Rubin recalls. "I asked the boy to stop playing basketball. He stopped, but then came out with his father and started [playing] again." Rubin grabbed a garden hose and, according to a legal complaint filed by the Schilds, soaked the boy and his father.

The Schilds sued Rubin and petitioned the court to grant a restraining order[7] against the Rubin family. The Schilds also claimed the emotional distress was so intense that they needed therapy. Rubin countersued the Schilds.

According to Rubin, many of the lawsuits have now been thrown out of court, but the ugly feelings still abound.

What can neighbors do to avoid this legal and emotional warfare? In a case involving a neighbor's child, it pays to be especially careful. "Realize that people are hypersensitive and defensive about their kids," says attorney Mark Warda. Instead of reacting in the heat of the moment, think about how you want to resolve the problem, and *then* calmly approach your neighbors.

Trees From the perspective of nuisance law, trees are one of the trickiest neighbor problems to resolve. That's because they serve so many vital purposes to a homeowner. They may be used for privacy, shade, fences, boundary markers or even food. So, in the case of a problem tree, be prepared to compromise.

That's something Evelyn King,* a thirty-two-year-old housewife in Connecticut, wishes she had done. Every autumn, Evelyn collected the several bushels of apples that had dropped from her neighbor's trees into her yard, to make cider. But last year, her neighbor approached her with a bill. "The tree belongs to me," he said. "If you want to use my apples, you have to pay for them."

The apple controversy raged on. Finally, Evelyn trimmed the apple-tree branches that hung over her property line. "My neighbor hired a tree consultant who claimed the trees were traumatized,"[8] she says.

Evelyn decided to build a high fence along her property line. "Now the neighbor calls me up to complain about the fence," she says. Even worse, the branches have started to grow back over her yard.

She could have avoided these troubles by making some concessions to her neighbor. For instance, she might have suggested that she'd be willing to allow the branches to hang over her

---

6. alienates (AY/lee/uh/nayts) makes unfriendly; turns away

7. restraining order a legal order that forbids a particular act until a court rules on the matter

*Name has been changed.

8. traumatized (TROW/muh/tyzd) given a damaging shock

property—and forgo the cider—if her neighbor would remove the apples that fell into her yard.

Declaring a Truce

Unfortunately, some neighbors are not willing to be reasonable. Instead, they become threatening, even violent.

In such cases, the ideal solution may be to bring in a neutral third party to mediate. Community or volunteer mediators charge a nominal fee (usually a total of $5 to $20) to help both parties reach a compromise. Suggest the idea to your uncooperative neighbor; if he refuses to participate, tell him your only other option is to call the police.

Neighbor mediation has become remarkably successful. The Dispute Resolution Section of the American Bar Association reports that over a quarter of a million neighbors underwent two-hour mediation sessions last year. Of those, 80 percent reached a satisfactory written agreement. And 95 percent of mediated agreements are currently being complied[9] with, more than twice the compliance rate of court-ordered resolutions.

---

9. complied (kum/PLYD) obeyed; acted in agreement with a request or command

Mediation helped Ann Drinkward and her neighbor finally solve their feud. "We found out information about each other that reduced the hostility," says Ann. "I didn't realize [the neighbor] was lonely." She promised to repair the damage her tree roots had caused. The neighbor, she says, agreed to come to her with complaints instead of taking irrational action.

Today, Ann feels emotionally entrenched in her neighborhood again. "I feel very secure now," she says. "I have my sense of belonging and place back."

For More Information

To find a mediator in your area, check the Yellow Pages of your phone book under "mediation services." Or contact:

- The National Institute for Dispute Resolution
  1726 M Street, N.W., Suite 500
  Washington, D.C. 20036-4502
  Phone: (202) 466-4764; Fax: (202) 466-4769
- Section of Dispute Resolution
  American Bar Association
  740 Fifteenth St., Washington, D.C. 20009
  Phone: (202) 662-1680; Fax: (202) 662-1683

▶ **Revisit Your Strategy: Use Your Prior Experience**
Check all the situations you or someone you know has had experience with.

_____ Barking neighborhood dogs

_____ Problems with boundary trees

_____ Constant complainers

_____ Inconsiderate neighbors

_____ Loud music

_____ Loud neighbors

_____ Neighbor mediation

_____ People who have sued neighbors

_____ Neighbors who become angrier because they are afraid to discuss a problem

_____ Neighbors whose parked cars block your way

_____ Obnoxious odors

_____ "Spite" fences

_____ Damage done by children or pets

Every experience you checked gave you insight into what the neighbors in the article may have felt or thought when they reacted as they did.

After You Read

A. Comprehension Check

1. About 45 percent of legal misdemeanor charges result from
   (1) "spite" fences   (3) excessive noise
   (2) vandalism   (4) neighbor disputes

2. When someone has a problem with a neighbor, his or her first impulse is usually to
   (1) file a lawsuit
   (2) avoid talking with the neighbor about the problem
   (3) yell at or insult the neighbor
   (4) destroy the neighbor's property

3. A person who has a problem with a neighbor child should
   (1) discipline the child
   (2) ignore the problem
   (3) build a fence
   (4) discuss the problem with the child's parents

4. A good way to deal with unreasonable neighbors is to
   (1) sue them   (3) bring in a mediator
   (2) leave them alone   (4) get a restraining order

5. When the author says, "remember that noise is subjective," we can infer that he thinks that
   (1) most people enjoy loud music
   (2) people have different feelings about noise
   (3) only loud noises are irritating
   (4) people shouldn't complain about loud music

6. When the author tells us that we treat our neighbors as family because of their sheer *proximity, proximity* means
   (1) closeness   (3) relationship
   (2) position   (4) familiarity

B. Read between the Lines

Check each statement that the author might agree with.

_____ 1. If a neighbor does something that annoys you, you can assume he did it on purpose.

_____ 2. If small annoyances build up, they can grow into major disputes.

_____ 3. You can avoid problems with your neighbors by doing nothing to annoy them.

_____ 4. Getting to know more about a troublesome neighbor may help solve problems between you.

_____ 5. With some neighbors, if one dispute is settled, they'll soon find something else to fight about.

_____ 6. If you confront your neighbors when you are angry, they'll see how upset you are and they won't repeat the offense.

C. Think beyond the Reading

Discuss these questions with a partner. Answer them in writing on separate paper if you wish.

1. Do you think the solutions suggested in this article would resolve neighbor disputes most of the time? Why or why not?

2. Look back at the answers you wrote for questions 2 and 3 in Before You Read on page 88. What changes, if any, would you make to those answers?

Think About It: Analyze Problems and Solutions

A **problem** is something that needs to be solved, and a **solution** is what solves it. The author of "The Neighbors from Hell" describes some problems that neighbors have experienced and their attempts to solve the problems. A standard problem-solving process, such as this one, might have helped them:

Step 1. State the problem.
Step 2. Identify the cause.
Step 3. Think of possible solutions.
Step 4. Evaluate the possible solutions and choose the best one.
Step 5. Develop a plan to carry out the solution and follow it.

A. Look at Problems and Solutions

Reread the first part of the article on page 89 and the last part on page 92 telling about the Drinkwards' problems with their neighbor. Here are the steps the Drinkwards took to solve their problems.

Step 1. State the problem: For 15 years we've had trouble with our next-door neighbor.
Step 2. Identify the cause: He finds fault with absurdly small things and reacts in ways that are annoying and even embarrassing.
Step 3. Think of possible solutions:
    Solution 1: Ignore him and the problem will go away.
    Solution 2: Be friendly; take him home-baked gifts.
    Solution 3: Meet with a mediator.
Step 4. Evaluate the possible solutions and choose the best one:
    Solution 1: We tried ignoring him, and it didn't work.
    Solution 2: It worked for a while, but the problems came back.
    Solution 3: Meeting with a mediator may make him act more reasonably.
    Choose the best one: Solution 3

Now complete Step 5 as you think the Drinkwards did:
Step 5. Develop a plan to carry out the solution and follow it.

_____

_____

The Drinkwards first had to convince the neighbor to join them in meeting with the mediator. Then they were able to understand their neighbor's loneliness and work out a better relationship.

Tip One good way to evaluate a solution is to ask, "Is this solution a remedy for the cause of the problem?

B. Practice

1. Reread the excerpt and complete the steps the man might have taken.

▶ In one California town, a man was so enraged by persistent barking from his neighbor's dog that he taped shut the pet's mouth. The dog died, and the man now faces criminal charges for animal cruelty.

Step 1. State the problem: The man is enraged by the neighbor's dog.
Step 2. Identify the cause: The dog barks constantly.
Step 3. Think of possible solutions.
    Solution 1: Ignore it.
    Solution 2: Tape the dog's mouth shut.
    Solution 3: Talk with the neighbors about how much it bothers you.
Step 4. Evaluate the possible solutions and choose the best one.

Solution 1: _____

Solution 2: _____

Solution 3: _____

Choose the best one: _____

Fill in a plan that might have worked out better for everyone:
Step 5. Develop a plan to carry out the solution and follow it.

_____

_____

2. Reread the following excerpts from "The Neighbors from Hell." Then on separate paper do the five-step problem-solving process to find a plan that might have worked out better for all concerned.

a. ▶ In a Connecticut neighborhood, when a family refused to trim their messy weeping-willow tree, someone drilled holes in the tree's trunk and poisoned it.

b. ▶ In 1989, Rubin's neighbors, the Schilds, erected a basketball hoop for their son about thirty feet from Rubin's bedroom window. One day, "I was so exhausted from work, I had to take a nap," Rubin recalls. "I asked the boy to stop playing basketball. He stopped, but then came out with his father and started [playing] again." Rubin grabbed a garden hose and, according to a legal complaint filed by the Schilds, soaked the boy and his father.

    ▶ **Talk About It**
    With a partner, compile a list of Good Neighbor tips that might help neighbors deal with problems before they get out of control.

Write About It: Write a Problem/Solution Essay

In "The Neighbors from Hell," the author describes some problems between neighbors and the solutions the neighbors tried. Then he suggests better solutions to the original problems. In this section, you will have a chance to write a problem/solution essay about a neighbor dispute. First study the sample, which shows how to write a problem/ solution essay.

Study the Sample

Read the steps below to see what the writer considered as she developed her essay.

Step 1: Picking a Topic. The writer picked as her topic an inconsiderate neighbor who did not follow laundry room etiquette.

Step 2: Developing and Organizing the Essay. The writer used the problem-solving process to organize her ideas. Then she suggested a better solution to the problem.

State the problem: Apartment house residents had to wait to use the washers and dryers in the laundry room.

Identify the cause: Mindy Lance was leaving clothes in the washers and dryers.

Think of possible solutions:
Solution 1: Take her clothes out of the washer and dryer and dump them in a corner.
Solution 2: Write letters of complaint and post them on the walls.
Solution 3: Inform the building manager and let her handle it.

Evaluate the possible solutions:
Solution 1: Someone tried this and started a battle of letters.
Solution 2: Letters just enraged the residents.
Solution 3: Letting the building manager handle it would have been better.

Choose the best solution: The building manager could have informed the residents that clothes should be removed from the washers and dryers promptly and that residents who routinely did not comply would not have their leases renewed.

Now read the sample essay on the next page. Then it will be your turn.

Your Turn

A. Prewriting

Step 1: The topics listed below may remind you of a neighbor dispute you know of. Select one, or think of one of your own.

- neighbors' children
- neighbors' pets
- neighbors who don't return borrowed things
- neighbors' loud music or yelling

Flare-Up in the Laundry Room

When you live in an apartment building, where only a wall separates you from your neighbors, everyone needs to be considerate of each other. That's not what happened in my apartment building.

Someone was always leaving her clothes in the washers and dryers in the laundry room. I got tired of running up and down the stairs to see if the clothes had been removed so I could start my own wash. Obviously, someone else got tired of it too, because one day someone took clothes from a washer and dryer and dumped them in a corner. This act started a battle of letters posted on the wall of the laundry room.

The first letter was from Mindy Lance, who was furious that her clothes had been removed from the washer and dryer and dumped. "The least you could have done," she wrote, "was put the dry clothes on the folding table and put the wet clothes in the dryer." She then threatened to dump anybody else's clothes she herself found in a washer or dryer.

Mindy Lance's letter enraged other residents, and they posted letters to her. One neighbor asked, "Since when do you have the right to make others wait hours for a washer, a dryer, or even the folding table, for that matter?" Another neighbor wrote that he was "really annoyed by people like you, who think you own the building." Eventually, Mindy began behaving properly, but hard feelings remained.

The problem could have been resolved better. If residents had informed the building manager, she then could have informed all residents that clothes should be removed from the washers and dryers within 15 minutes after their wash was done. Those who refused to comply would not have their leases renewed. That would have been a fair, commonsense solution. Neighbor problems may sometimes seem inevitable, especially in an apartment building, but it's important to resolve them fairly.

Step 2: Describe your chosen problem, its cause, and its solution. You might want to use a step-by-step process like the one on page 96. If there was a better solution than the one tried, describe it.

B. Writing

On separate paper, write your essay.

 Tip Add an introduction that sets up the problem situation and a conclusion that wraps up its solution.

▶ **Save your draft.** At the end of this unit, you will work with one of your drafts further.

Lesson 8

LEARNING GOALS

Strategy: Summarize
Reading: Read workplace training information
Skill: Apply ideas
Writing: Write a solution to a problem

Before You Read

Making sure customers are happy is good business. Even in the best-run businesses, there will be customers who become upset about the service or merchandise they have received. Employees who come in contact with the public need to know how to handle these difficult situations. "Calming Upset Customers" outlines some principles for dealing with upset customers. Before you read the selection, think about a time when you were an upset customer trying to complain to an employee. What could the employee have done to make you a happy customer? Check the appropriate statements below.

I would have been a happy customer if the employee had

_____ **1.** listened to me and not interrupted

_____ **2.** not argued with me

_____ **3.** agreed with me that there was a problem

_____ **4.** treated me with respect

_____ **5.** taken my complaint seriously

_____ **6.** immediately suggested a way to resolve the problem

_____ **7.** offered to pay me for my wasted time and energy

_____ **8.** taken steps to be sure the problem would not be repeated in the future

_____ **9.** other: _____

Preview the Reading

Read the title and the headings to learn what topics are covered in the article.

Set Your Strategy: Summarize

To **summarize** means to restate briefly the main idea and most important supporting details in a reading selection. As you read "Calming Upset Customers," think about the main points discussed. You may want to highlight them, underline them, or take notes to remember them. When you are finished reading the selection, you will have a chance to complete a statement summarizing the information.

Calming Upset Customers

Rebecca L. Morgan

WHAT DO UPSET CUSTOMERS WANT?

THE CUSTOMER WANTS . . .

To be taken seriously

The customer does not want a response like "You're kidding," "No way" or "You've got to be joking." He wants you to be professional and confident and to respond seriously to his concern.

To be treated with respect

The upset person doesn't want condescension[1] or arrogance. She wants you to treat her and her concern with respect. This may be difficult when the customer is clearly at fault but is trying to blame your organization.

Immediate action

He doesn't want you to look into it next month, next week, or even tomorrow. He wants you to do something *now*. Show you are concerned by moving briskly, no matter how tired you are.

Compensation[2]/restitution[3]

He wants someone to pay for the damage done, and perhaps for his time, inconvenience, or pain.

Someone to be reprimanded[4] and/or punished

Assure the customer that corrective action will be taken, even if you aren't the supervisor. Discreetly report the incident to the supervisor so she can explain the problem to your co-worker and avoid similar problems in the future.

To clear up the problem so it never happens again

Sometimes the customer just wants to know that some action has been put in motion, so that no one will have this problem again. Assure her you will report the problem to the person who can take care of it.

Reprinted with permission. "Calming Upset Customers". Crisp Publications, Inc., 1200 Hamilton Court, Menlo Park, California 94025; 800-442-7477.

Calming Upset Customers

1. **condescension** (kon/di/SEN/shun) an attitude of superiority
2. **compensation** (kom/pen/SAY/shun) payment to make up for an injury or loss
3. **restitution** (res/tuh/TOO/shun) making up for an injury or loss by restoring or giving something equal in value
4. **reprimanded** (REH/prih/man/did) formally criticized and blamed

To be listened to

What the upset customer wants first is to be listened to. It is difficult to listen carefully in a tense situation, especially if you have not developed effective listening habits.

Why don't we listen well? What habits do you think prevent people from listening fully, especially in stressful situations?

_____

_____

_____

LISTENING HABITS

According to Dr. Lyman K. Steil, President of Communication Development, in St. Paul, Minnesota, most people have poor listening habits. Some of the habits Dr. Steil has discovered are:

Criticizing the speaker and delivery

Focusing not on what the speaker is saying, but how she is saying it. Noticing a lisp, a stutter, an accent, a dialect, grammatical errors, "uns" and "uhs"—rather than the speaker's thoughts and feelings.

Listening only for facts and not for feelings

A customer may not *say* he's angry, but his voice conveys it loudly and clearly. Listen carefully for emotions as well as facts.

Not taking notes—or trying to write down everything

Not taking notes can cause problems later, when you try to remember what was said. On the other hand, trying to take down everything the customer says will make you lose all eye contact. Take a few brief notes of important details, like dates, times, amounts, and account numbers.

Faking attention

Customers can quickly discern if you are paying attention to them or not. If she was mildly agitated[5] before, your inattention can push her into anger. Pay close attention when you are helping her.

Tuning out difficult or confusing information

When people are upset they don't always communicate clearly. If you habitually tune out what you don't immediately understand, practice pleasantly asking the person to slow down. It's easier to understand information one piece at a time. Take notes to help you put the pieces together.

Reprinted with permission. "Calming Upset Customers". Crisp Publications, Inc., 1200 Hamilton Court, Menlo Park, California 94025; 800-442-7477.

Calming Upset Customers

5. agitated (A/jih/tay/tid) disturbed or upset

Letting emotional words block the message

The upset customer may call you names, curse, or say unpleasant things about you, your co-workers, and your organization. Avoid letting him "push your buttons" in this way, because when you're upset you've lost objectivity, and you need to be in control if you're going to find a solution to this situation.

Interrupting or finishing the other person's sentences

This is an irritating habit and will only induce more anger in an already upset person.

Biases[6] and prejudices

We all have biases and prejudices, whether we like to admit it or not. You may not like the way someone dresses, her makeup, his hair style, or her stutter. It is hard to listen when you're distracted by these biases. Work on eliminating your prejudices so as to be a better listener.

Not facing the upset person

Look her in the eye. Remember what your parents said when you were a kid: "Look at me when I'm talking to you." People see you are listening when you are looking at them.

Not checking that you've understood

Repeat what you understand the customer to be saying. Start your sentence with "Let's see if I understand . . ." or "I think I understand . . ." (then paraphrase[7] what she said). Don't say "What you're trying to say is . . ."—it implies the customer is an idiot and can't say what he means. Also avoid "What I hear you saying is . . ."—it's overused and trite.

WORDS TO WATCH

Here are some words that can be annoying and words that are more neutral—Fight Starters and Communication Helpers. Fight Starters are words to avoid—because they'll enrage someone who's already upset. Communication Helpers are alternatives that will help to calm the person down.

Use verbal cushions—show empathy

Verbal cushions let the customer know that you can understand why she would be upset. You're not saying you know exactly how she feels, because you can't know that.

You're also acknowledging his right to feel that way. You're not pooh-poohing his feelings.

Calming Upset Customers

Reprinted with permission. "Calming Upset Customers". Crisp Publications, Inc., 1200 Hamilton Court, Menlo Park, California 94025; 800-442-7477.

6. **biases** (BY/ah/sez) prejudices; strong leanings for or against something
7. **paraphrase** (PA/ruh/frayz) restate the meaning of something using other words

Fight Starters:	*Communication Helpers:*
You're crazy.	I can appreciate what you're saying.
I know how you feel.	I can understand how you'd feel that way.
	I can understand how that would be annoying.
Boy, you're sure mad.	I can see how you'd be upset.
I don't know why you're so upset.	I would be upset too.
	It sounds as if we've caused you inconvenience. I'm sorry.

Use the 3 F's: Feel, Felt, Found

The 3 F's are a skeleton on which to hang the rest of your response. This technique acknowledges the customer's feelings and offers an explanation in a way she can listen to:

"I understand how you could <u>feel</u> that way.
Others have <u>felt</u> that way too.
And then they <u>found</u>, after an explanation, that this policy protected them, so it made sense."

Get clarification

Paraphrase what he is saying. Take the blame if there is a miscommunication. Make sure you understand the concern before you try to solve it.

Fight Starters:	*Communication Helpers:*
You're way off base.	What it sounds like you're saying . . .
You aren't making any sense.	Maybe I misunderstood . . .
That's definitely wrong.	Let me see if I've got this straight . . .
Did you really say . . .	Here's what I understood you to say . . .

Form a team

Let her know her patronage[8] is important. When you form a team it is the two of you together working on a solution, rather than Her vs. You.

Fight Starters:	*Communication Helpers:*
We can't do that.	I want to help find a solution.
<u>You</u> sure have a problem.	Let's see what we can work out together.

Reprinted with permission. "Calming Upset Customers". Crisp Publications, Inc., 1200 Hamilton Court, Menlo Park, California 94025; 800-442-7477.

Calming Upset Customers

---

8. patronage (PA/truh/nij) business given by regular customers

ADDITIONAL POINTERS

Time Out

If you find yourself becoming upset, wanting to cry, or to yell at the customer, allow yourself a little time away from the situation. This will give you a chance to calm down before you return to the fray.[9]

When you know you're getting emotional, excuse yourself politely:

"Excuse me a moment while I check the policy on this."
"I'd like to get my supervisor's opinion on this."
"I need to verify some information in the file."
"I need to discuss how we can best solve this. I'll be just a moment."

Always excuse yourself in a way that shows your interest in serving the customer.

How to Get the Customer's Attention

If the customer is ranting and not giving you a chance to explain or ask questions, use his or her name at the beginning of your sentence. Most people listen when they hear their name.

If the Customer Is Obstinate[10]. . .

If you are having trouble reaching an agreement, make comments that direct the customer toward finding a solution:

"What would you like me to do now?"
"What do you think is a fair way to settle this?"
"What would make you happy?"

Often, what she will ask for is less than you might have offered. If the customer's proposal is within your guidelines, accept it. If not, make a counterproposal.

If you can't reach an agreement, it's time to call in your boss. Unless you are a manager, it is not your place to invite a customer to take her business elsewhere.

Polite Repetition

If the customer keeps insisting on something that's unreasonable or impossible, tell him what you can do (not what you can't do). Keep repeating it, without becoming hostile or loud, until you're finally heard. For example, if the customer insists on getting a widget, and you have none in stock, the conversation might go like this:

Calming Upset Customers

---

9. fray a noisy quarrel or disagreement
10. obstinate (OB/stuh/nit) not giving in; stubborn

"I want my widget today."
"I'm sorry, we will have more widgets in on Tuesday."
"But I need it today."
"I'm sorry, we don't have any in stock."
"I want it today."
"I'll be glad to get one to you on Tuesday."

Eventually, you may have to ask him to leave. If he won't, then call in the security guards or the police.

Dealing with Violence

There may be occasions when an enraged customer threatens you, or becomes violent. Rely on your gut feeling if it seems things are getting out of hand. Learn to look for potentially violent behavior by reading the nonverbal communication of the customer—clenched fists, tight lips, agitated tone of voice, tense body posture, flared nostrils, red face, and wide-open eyes. Look for evidence of drugs or alcohol.

If the customer becomes unruly, or threatens violence, seek assistance. You do not have to put up with threats.

Never try to reason with a drunk or a drug user. Even if there's no sign of drugs, if the person appears potentially violent, don't feel stupid about calling the police. There are plenty of stories about employees being punched by upset customers. It's better to risk feeling stupid than to end up in the hospital.

Never accuse a customer of being drunk or on drugs. This can put you and your company in a liable[11] situation. Find another way to assist the customer out of your establishment.

Reprinted with permission. "Calming Upset Customers". Crisp Publications, Inc., 1200 Hamilton Court, Menlo Park, California 94025; 800-442-7477.

Calming Upset Customers

---

11. **liable** (LY/ah/bul) legally obligated or responsible

▶ **Revisit Your Strategy: Summarize**
Complete the statement below to summarize the article "Calming Upset Customers."

An upset customer may calm down when _____

_____

_____

After You Read

A. Comprehension Check

1. Most customers want each of the following *except*
   (1) a joking response from an employee
   (2) respect
   (3) immediate help
   (4) an employee who listens

2. According to Dr. Steil, customers think an employee is listening when the employee
   (1) doesn't take notes
   (2) asks the customer to slowly explain the problem
   (3) finishes the customer's sentences
   (4) tries to write everything down

3. Which of the following is a Fight Starter?
   (1) I can see how you'd be upset.
   (2) You're very upset.
   (3) I would be upset too.
   (4) I understand why you're upset.

4. To avoid getting upset when dealing with an angry customer, you should
   (1) call the manager
   (2) ask the customer to leave
   (3) tell the customer to calm down
   (4) politely excuse yourself for a short time

5. In the sentence "if it seems things are getting out of hand . . . look for *potentially* violent behavior . . . ," *potentially* means
   (1) extremely   (3) possibly
   (2) suddenly   (4) unlikely

6. Based on the article, if you get in an argument with an angry person, you should
   (1) ignore most of what she's saying
   (2) avoid eye contact
   (3) speak calmly and show you're concerned
   (4) tell her she's way out of line

B. Read between the Lines

Check each term that describes the qualities a good customer relations worker would have. Look back at the selection to find support for each description you check.

_____ reassuring	_____ strong-willed	_____ sincere
_____ patient	_____ lighthearted	_____ dominating
_____ fault-finding	_____ understanding	_____ good at listening
_____ capable	_____ respectful	_____ cool under fire

C. Think beyond the Reading

Discuss these questions with a partner. Answer them in writing on separate paper if you wish.

1. Do you think some of the information in the selection could also be helpful to someone dealing with an upset co-worker, friend, or spouse? Why or why not?
2. Look back at the list of solutions in Before You Read on page 98. How would thinking about your own experiences as an upset customer help you calm angry customers you meet as an employee?

Think About It: Apply Ideas

"Calming Upset Customers" suggests many ideas for employees to use when dealing with angry customers. Now think about how you might **apply the ideas** in some specific situations.

A. Look at Applying Ideas

Review these general ideas from "Calming Upset Customers."

The customer wants . . .

- To be taken seriously
- To be treated with respect
- Immediate action
- Compensation/restitution

Suppose you are a restaurant manager and an angry customer waves you over and says, "We've been waiting half an hour for our food. Where is it? And where's our waiter?" The chart below lists the four general ideas that employees can use to calm an upset customer. Then it gives examples of how to apply three of the ideas to this situation. Complete the chart with a final example.

Idea	One way you could apply the idea
Take the customer seriously.	Have a serious, concerned expression.
Treat the customer with respect.	Address the customer as "Sir" or "Ma'am."
Take immediate action.	Say, "I'll see what the problem is," and go directly to the kitchen or wait station.
See if compensation is possible.	_____

You may have suggested reducing the customer's bill, or perhaps a free dessert, or a $5 or $10 coupon off their next dinner. All those suggestions apply the idea of compensation.

 Tip   When you read an idea that you may want to apply, think of a situation when you might use the idea and imagine what you would say or do in that situation.

B. Practice

1. Suppose you are a salesperson in an appliance store. A customer is upset because his brand-new refrigerator stopped working. He walks into the store and begins to yell at the first salesperson he sees—you. Complete the chart below. For each general idea, write an example of how to apply it in this situation.

Idea	One way you could apply the idea
Verbally cushion the customer's concerns.	
Probe for more information; get clarification.	
Take immediate action.	
See if compensation is possible.	

2. Suppose while playing ball your sons have damaged your neighbor's shrubs. Your neighbor is angry. Below are some ideas from the article "Calming Upset Customers." On separate paper, make a chart like the one above. Choose four or five ideas from the list below and write an example of how to apply each idea to the conflict with your neighbor.

- Treat the problem seriously.
- Treat the neighbor with respect.
- Apologize for the situation.
- Listen carefully.
- Use verbal cushions.
- Avoid Fight Starters.
- Take immediate action.

- Offer compensation.
- Probe for more information.
- Ask what he'd like to have happen.
- Promise the boys will be reprimanded or punished.
- Clear up the problem so it doesn't happen again.

3. With a partner, role-play the situation in question 1 or 2 above. The partner playing the employee or parent should apply as many ideas from the reading as possible.

▶ **Talk About It**

"Calming Upset Customers" provides ideas for employees to use when dealing with angry customers. Perhaps angry customers should have a similar guide to use when they complain to employees. With a partner, prepare a list of ideas that could help angry customers state their complaints clearly and effectively. Then combine all the ideas into a master list of tips on how to stay calm when you are upset.

Write About It: Write a Solution to a Problem

"Calming Upset Customers" lists ideas for dealing with angry customers. In this section, you will have a chance to write a solution to a problem you had as a customer. First study the sample, which shows how to write a solution to a problem.

Study the Sample

Read the steps below to see what the writer considered as he developed his solution.

Step 1: Picking a Topic. The writer of the sample wrote the following topic sentence to help guide his development of ideas: I wasted a half day of vacation time waiting for an electrician who never showed up and talking with a rude receptionist.

Step 2: Developing and Organizing the Solution. The writer listed the details of his problem in chronological order. He also noted ideas from "Calming Upset Customers" that could have been used to handle the problem better.

How the problem was handled	How it could have been handled better
After waiting until noon for an electrician who was supposed to be there "first thing in the morning," I was told he was probably still at another job.	Take the complaint seriously. Show respect and concern.
The receptionist responded to me casually and seemed unconcerned.	Use verbal cushions—show empathy.
She told me other people also had problems and didn't seem to care whether mine got fixed.	Form a team so you can work together on a solution.
She finally offered to send the electrician in the evening at no extra cost.	Take immediate action. Offer restitution.

Now read the sample problem and solution on the next page. Then it will be your turn.

Your Turn

A. Prewriting

Step 1: Choose a topic. Think of a time when you were a customer whose complaint was handled poorly. Write a sentence introducing the topic:

_____

Step 2: List the details on how the problem was handled on separate paper. Also list ideas from "Calming Upset Customers" on how the problem could have been handled better.

How *Not* to Handle an Angry Customer

Electrical problems are never fun. Here I was, sitting in the gloom of my quiet living room, waiting for the electrician to come and fix my problem. I had called the evening before, as soon as half my house had been plunged into darkness, and I was promised an electrician would be out the first thing in the morning. I had arranged with my boss to take half a vacation day from work. But it was now ten minutes to noon. And no electrician. I decided to call the repair service again.

"Where is he?" I tried not to yell at the receptionist. "You promised he'd be here first thing in the morning. I've been sitting here the whole morning waiting for him."

"He's probably still at another job," she said casually.

"He was supposed to be *here* first thing in the morning. Why did he go somewhere else?" I demanded to know.

"Well, other people have electrical problems too, you know," she responded.

"Look, there must be something you can do to help me. I have to go to work now. I wasted half a vacation day sitting here waiting! And my power is still off. Isn't there anything you can do?"

"Well, I could page him and tell him to go to your place this evening, if you'd like," she finally offered.

"At no extra overtime cost?" I asked.

"Uh, all right. At no extra overtime cost."

"That would be great! I'll be home by five-thirty," I said.

The receptionist could have handled the situation better. When I first told her I was waiting for an electrician the whole morning, she should have acknowledged that I had a right to be upset. She also should have apologized for my inconvenience and immediately offered to send the electrician in the evening. Her poor handling of this problem cost her company a repeat customer and a good reference.

B. Writing

On separate paper, describe your problem and tell how it was handled. Then offer a better solution.

Tip Before you write your solution, put yourself in the employee's position to make sure your solution would be agreeable to *both* sides.

▶ **Save your draft.** At the end of this unit, you will work with one of your drafts further.

Lesson 9

LEARNING GOALS

Strategy: Imagine
Reading: Read an essay
Skill: Analyze a writer's craft
Writing: Write a personal experience essay

Before You Read

Robert Fulghum has written several best-selling books, including *All I Really Need to Know I Learned in Kindergarten.* In "Summer of 1959," the essay in this lesson, Fulghum describes a time when, as a young man, he was so upset about his working conditions that he lost his temper and almost quit his job. He tells how he learned a valuable lesson.

Before you read the essay, think about things that have upset you or someone you know at work or in daily life. List two or three things, and write how they made you feel and what you did about them. Did you lose your temper? Did someone intervene to help you calm down? Did the problem get solved to your satisfaction?

_____

_____

_____

_____

Preview the Reading

Read the introduction, the title, and the author's name. Look at the illustration. Then read the first paragraph of the essay. Does the author's style tell you something about what to expect from this reading?

Set Your Strategy: Imagine

When you **imagine** as you read, you try to see, hear, feel, and think the way the people in the story do. You use details to visualize, forming a mental picture of the characters, the setting, and the events described by the author. As you read about the people, places, and events in the following essay, try to imagine them. When you finish reading the essay, you will have a chance to tell how you imagined they looked, sounded, felt, and thought.

Some people are easily upset when things don't go their way.
In this essay, the author tells how he reacted when he disagreed rather
violently with his boss and what he learned from the experience.

Summer of 1959

Robert Fulghum

In the summer of 1959. At the Feather River Inn near the town of Blairsden in the Sierra Nevada Mountains of northern California. A resort environment. And I, just out of college, have a job that combines being the night desk clerk in the lodge and helping out with the horse-wrangling at the stables. The owner/manager is Italian-Swiss, with European notions about conditions of employment. He and I do not get along. I think he's a fascist[1] who wants peasant employees who know their place, and he thinks I'm a good example of how democracy can be carried too far. I'm twenty-two and pretty free with my opinions, and he's fifty-two and has a few opinions of his own.

One week the employees had been served the same thing for lunch every single day. Two wieners, a mound of sauerkraut, and stale rolls. To compound insult with injury, the cost of meals was deducted from our check. I was outraged.

On Friday night of that awful week, I was at my desk job around 11:00 P.M., and the night auditor[2] had just come on duty. I went into the kitchen to get a bite to eat and saw notes to the chef to the effect that wieners and sauerkraut are on the employee menu for two more days.

That tears it. I quit! For lack of any better audience, I unloaded on the night auditor, Sigmund Wollman. I declared that I have had it up to here; that I am going to get a plate of wieners and sauerkraut and go and wake up the owner and throw it on him. I am sick and tired of this crap and insulted and nobody is going to make me eat wieners and sauerkraut for a whole week and make me pay for it and who does he think he is anyhow and how can life be sustained on wieners and sauerkraut and this is un-American and I don't like wieners and sauerkraut enough to eat it one day for God's sake and the whole hotel stinks

---

1. **fascist** (FASH/ist) one who supports a government ruled by a dictator

2. **auditor** (AW/dih/ter) someone authorized to verify business accounts

anyhow and the horses are all nags and the guests are all idiots and I'm packing my bags and heading for Montana where they never even heard of wieners and sauerkraut and wouldn't feed that stuff to pigs. Something like that. I'm still mad about it.

I raved on in this way for twenty minutes, and needn't repeat it all here. You get the drift. My monologue was delivered at the top of my lungs, punctuated by blows on the front desk with a fly-swatter, the kicking of chairs, and much profanity. A call to arms, freedom, unions, uprisings, and the breaking of chains for the working masses.

As I pitched my fit, Sigmund Wollman, the night auditor, sat quietly on his stool, smoking a cigarette, watching me with sorrowful eyes. Put a bloodhound in a suit and tie and you have Sigmund Wollman. He's got good reason to look sorrowful. Survivor of Auschwitz.[3] Three years. German Jew. Thin, coughed a lot. He liked being alone at the night job—gave him intellectual space, gave him peace and quiet, and, even more, he could go into the kitchen and have a snack whenever he wanted to—all the wieners and sauerkraut he wanted. To him, a feast. More than that, there's nobody around at night to tell him what to do. In Auschwitz he dreamed of such a time. The only person he sees at work is me, the nightly disturber of his dream. Our shifts overlap for an hour. And here I am again. A one-man war party at full cry.

"Fulchum[4], are you finished?"

"No. Why?"

"Lissen, Fulchum. Lissen me, lissen me. You know what's wrong with you? It's not wieners and kraut and it's not the boss and it's not the chef and it's not this job."

"So what's wrong with me?"

"Fulchum, you think you know everything, but you don't know the difference between an inconvenience[5] and a problem.

"If you break your neck, if you have nothing to eat, if your house is on fire—then you got a problem. Everything else is inconvenience. Life *is* inconvenient. Life *is* lumpy.

"Learn to separate the inconveniences from the real problems. You will live longer. And will not annoy people like me so much. Good night."

In a gesture combining dismissal and blessing, he waved me off to bed.

Seldom in my life have I been hit between the eyes with truth so hard. Years later I heard a Japanese Zen Buddhist priest describe what the moment of enlightenment was like and I knew exactly what he meant. There in that late-night darkness of the Feather River Inn, Sigmund Wollman simultaneously kicked my butt and opened a window in my mind.

For thirty years now, in times of stress and strain, when something has me backed against the wall and I'm ready to do something really stupid with my anger, a sorrowful face appears in my mind and asks: "Fulchum. Problem or inconvenience?"

I think of this as the Wollman Test of Reality. Life is lumpy. And a lump in the oatmeal, a lump in the throat, and a lump in a breast are not the same lump. One should learn the difference. Good night, Sig.

---

3. Auschwitz (OUSH/vits) site of a Nazi concentration camp in Poland where millions were killed during World War II

4. Fulchum the author's name spelled to indicate Wollman's mid-European accent

5. inconvenience (in/kun/VEE/nyunss) small trouble or annoyance

Revisit Your Strategy: Imagine
Write a few words or phrases describing how you imagined the author looked and sounded during his tantrum.

After You Read

A. Comprehension Check

1. The narrator is upset that
   (1) he is being fired
   (2) he has to eat wieners and sauerkraut every day for lunch
   (3) his boss is a fascist
   (4) the night auditor bothers him while he is trying to work

2. The narrator sees each of the following as a solution to his problem *except*
   (1) throwing wieners and sauerkraut on the owner
   (2) packing his bags and heading for Montana
   (3) quitting his job
   (4) feeding wieners and sauerkraut to pigs

3. According to Wollman, what's wrong with the narrator is that he
   (1) has a picky appetite
   (2) doesn't appreciate good food
   (3) doesn't understand what a real problem is
   (4) dislikes the chef

4. Wollman believes the narrator will live a longer life if he
   (1) learns to like what he's served
   (2) stops annoying people
   (3) does not get upset over little things
   (4) stops thinking he knows everything

5. Fulghum is being objective when he says,
   (1) "I think he's a fascist."
   (2) "The owner-manager is Italian-Swiss."
   (3) "The guests are all idiots."
   (4) "This is un-American."

6. When Fulghum says, "Sigmund Wollman simultaneously kicked my butt and opened a window in my mind," he is describing
   (1) having a moment of enlightenment
   (2) being dismissed from his job
   (3) being given a blessing
   (4) being in a concentration camp

B. Read between the Lines

Check the statements you think Sigmund Wollman would agree with.

_____ 1. Some things in life are not worth getting upset about.
_____ 2. A threat to your health is a real problem.
_____ 3. Not liking your boss is a real problem.
_____ 4. Having a college degree doesn't mean you know everything.
_____ 5. Not liking the food you are served is an inconvenience.
_____ 6. You should never protest against anything.

C. Think beyond the Reading

Discuss these questions with a partner. Answer them in writing on separate paper if you wish.

1. How can separating inconveniences from real problems help people resolve conflicts?
2. Look back at the things you listed in Before You Read on page 110. Would you classify them as problems or inconveniences? Why?

Think About It: Analyze a Writer's Craft

A **writer's craft** involves all the devices a writer uses to communicate ideas and emotions and increase the reader's involvement and enjoyment. In lessons 1 and 2, you learned about characterization and mood—two devices of a writer's craft. In "Summer of 1959," Fulghum uses several devices to capture your attention and keep you involved in his tale.

A. Look at Writer's Craft

See how the author grabs your interest right from the beginning.

▶ [1]In the summer of 1959. [2]At the Feather River Inn near the town of Blairsden in the Sierra Nevada Mountains of northern California. [3]A resort environment. [4]And I, just out of college, have a job that combines being the night desk clerk in the lodge and helping out with the horse-wrangling at the stables. [5]The owner/manager is Italian-Swiss, with European notions about conditions of employment. [6]He and I do not get along. [7]I think he's a fascist who wants peasant employees who know their place, and he thinks I'm a good example of how democracy can be carried too far. [8]I'm twenty-two and pretty free with my opinions, and he's fifty-two and has a few opinions of his own.

The chart below lists some of the devices Fulghum used to get you involved and make you want to read on. Complete the chart by listing the examples of the third method, comparing and contrasting ideas, and tell how you think it works.

Device	Examples	How It Works
Sentence fragments	sentences 1, 2, and 3	These short fragments catch our attention and propel us into the story.
Varied sentence construction	sentences 4 and 5	The variety changes the pace of the reading and keeps us interested.
Comparing and contrasting ideas	_____ _____	_____ _____

Sentences 6, 7, and 8 compare and contrast ideas. The two men are similar because they do not get along and have strong opinions. They are different in what they think of each other. The contrasting ideas prepare you for a conflict to come. Analyzing a writer's craft can help you better appreciate good writing.

Tip To analyze a writer's craft, think about how you felt as you read. Ask yourself what made you feel that way. Was it varied sentence length? Colorful language? Interesting details? Humor or exaggeration?

B. Practice

1. The point of highest tension in the essay comes in the fourth paragraph. Reread the sentence that begins "I am sick and tired . . ." and ends ". . . feed that slop to pigs."

   How did this run-on sentence make you feel? _____

   _____

2. Much of the humor in the essay is expressed through exaggeration. List an example of exaggeration found in each of these paragraphs:

   a. Paragraph 1: _____

   b. Paragraph 5: _____

3. Fulghum uses colorful language, particularly slang, to deliver a serious message in a light tone.

   List examples of colorful language in paragraphs 4 and 5: _____

   _____

4. The mood of the essay changes when Fulghum focuses attention on Wollman. List

   a few words and phrases he uses to characterize Wollman. _____

   _____

5. Writers strive for a strong ending. Reread the last paragraph. How did it make you

   feel? Do you think it is a strong ending? Why or why not? _____

   _____

6. Which of the devices below did the author use to craft the essay? Check all that apply.

_____ run-on sentences	_____ formal language	_____ humor
_____ slow pace	_____ colorful language	_____ exaggeration
_____ sentence fragments	_____ interesting details	_____ relaxed mood

   ▶ **Talk About It**
   In "Summer of 1959," Robert Fulghum loses his temper at work. Some people, when they lose their tempers, may even commit violence. Find articles in news-papers and magazines about violent acts people have committed to resolve conflicts. With a partner or small group, discuss and list ways the people might have dealt with their problems peacefully.

Write About It: Write a Personal Experience Essay

The author of "Summer of 1959" tells some advice he got from a co-worker about how to separate important from unimportant conflicts. Now you will have a chance to write an essay about an event from which you learned a lesson about life. First study the sample, which shows how to write a personal experience essay.

Study the Sample

Read the steps below to see what the writer considered as she developed her action plan.

Step 1: Picking a Topic. The writer of the essay chose this topic: what I learned about supervising co-workers.

Step 2: Developing and Organizing the Essay. Below is a work sheet on which the writer listed the events that happened to her and recorded how she felt about them. She ended the work sheet with a statement describing what she learned from the experience.

What happened	My feelings and thoughts at the time
Was promoted to shift floor manager at store	Felt proud
Needed to stock and do displays for big sale	Wanted to do a good job; pitched in and helped
One co-worker got little done	Wanted to be liked by co-workers; remembered Dad's "honey and vinegar" saying; figured I'd be nice about it
Co-worker went off to make phone call	Tried to be a little firmer
Saw display would not be arranged in time	Knew I had to get firm with worker
What I learned: Sometimes you need to be firm and not worry about whether people like you.	

Now read the writer's essay on the next page. Then it will be your turn.

Your Turn

A. Prewriting

Step 1: Pick a topic. Write about a situation from which you learned either how to handle a conflict or how to separate the important from the unimportant.

Step 2: Make a work sheet that lists the events that happened and your thoughts and feelings about them. Then state what you learned from the experience.

Sometimes Honey Doesn't Work

I worked for a large department store for two years, always on time, putting in long hours, doing a good job. So when I was promoted to floor manager of the second shift, I knew I had earned it, and I felt proud.

About a month after my promotion, the store had a huge weekend sale. My shift was responsible for arranging sales displays and making sure all the shelves were stocked. Thursday evening, I gave my co-workers their assignments. Then I pitched in and helped too, arranging a display in the shoe department. About five o'clock, I made the rounds to see how the others were coming along.

Imagine my surprise when I entered the sporting goods department and found it a mess! Baseball gloves, weights, fishing gear, golf bags—scattered everywhere. "Louis!" I said. "Where are you? What's going on?"

Louis emerged from behind an exercise machine. "Uh, I've been busy with customers," he said. "Can I go to dinner now?"

I wanted to shout, "What customers? Hardly anybody is in the store! They're all waiting for the sale!" But I remembered what my father had always told me: "You'll catch more flies with honey than with vinegar." I wanted my co-workers to like me. I smiled and said, "OK, Louis, you've got half an hour. But then get moving on these displays, OK?" I congratulated myself for being so understanding.

Two hours later, my father's saying had begun to wear thin. I went to the sporting goods department. Next to nothing had been accomplished. When I looked for Louis, I found him on the telephone in the break room. "Look, Louis," I said. "We really need those displays done by ten o'clock."

At eight o'clock, with only the fishing display done, I knew I had to get firm. "Louis, I'll help you finish displaying and stocking. But your lack of effort tonight is unacceptable. If it happens again, I'll write it in your file."

"Sure, I understand." And Louis worked harder than I'd ever seen him work before. I now think he was just testing me to see what he could get away with. I've learned that being liked by co-workers is not as important as being respected. Sometimes a little vinegar can be just what's required.

B. Writing

On separate paper, write an essay about the topic you selected.

Tip As you write your essay, think about the different devices you can use to capture your readers' attention. The writer of the sample essay wove her father's saying into the title and the concluding statement.

 Save your draft. At the end of this unit, you will work with one of your drafts further.

▶ Writing Skills Mini-Lesson: Subject-Verb Agreement

Verbs must agree with their subjects. If the subject is singular, the verb must be singular too. If the subject is plural, the verb must also be plural. Here are a few guidelines for some troublesome subjects.

1. **These words are always singular.** Words ending in *-one, -thing,* or *-body* are singular. So are *each, every,* and *much.*

   Everybody was at the meeting. **No one was** absent. (not *were*)
   Each of the board members **was** scheduled to speak. (not *were*)

2. **These words are always plural.** *Many, several, some, most, both,* and *few* are plural.

   Many have experienced conflicts at work. (not *has experienced*)
   Most are able to settle their conflicts peacefully. (not *is able*)
   Fortunately, **few become** violent. (not *becomes*)

3. **Collective nouns are usually singular.** Collective nouns are nouns that stand for a group or collection of people or things. Some examples are *audience, committee, company, crowd, group,* and *team.*

   The **company offers** a workshop every month. (not *offer*)

   - When a collective noun stands for a group as a whole, use a singular verb.
     Our **team is going** to attend Friday. (not *are going*)

   - When the individual members of the group are emphasized, use a plural verb.
     Our **team are going** to attend separate sessions next time.

Practice: Copy the paragraphs on separate paper. Make every verb agree with its subject.

> My company are offering three workshops. Each of the workshops are about a different kind of conflict. The first workshop is called "The Angry Customer." Everybody seem to have had a problem with a customer at one time or another. Most customers are polite, but a few loses control. A customer of mine once tried to return a shirt, but several of the buttons was missing. He shouted, "I want my money back," and started to push me. Luckily, one of the supervisors were nearby and came to my rescue.

> Employees are human too, and a few has begun shouting back. The work-shop is supposed to prevent such incidents. Everyone need a calm way to resolve conflicts with customers. The audience learn several ways to handle angry customers. My group are really looking forward to this workshop.

Conflict Strategies: What Are You Like?

David W. Johnson

Different people use different strategies for managing conflicts. These strategies are learned, usually in childhood, and they seem to function automatically. Usually we are not aware of how we act in conflict situations. We just do whatever seems to come naturally. But we do have a personal strategy, and because it was learned, we can always change it by learning new and more effective ways of managing conflicts.

When you become engaged in a conflict, there are two major concerns you have to take into account:

1. Achieving your personal goals—you are in conflict because you have a goal that conflicts with another person's goal. Your goal may be highly important to you, or it may be of little importance.
2. Keeping a good relationship with the other person—you may need to be able to interact effectively with the other person in the future. The relationship may be very important to you, or it may be of little importance.

How important your personal goals are to you and how important the relationship is to you affect how you act in a conflict. Given these two concerns, five styles of managing conflicts can be identified:

1. *The Turtle* (Withdrawing). Turtles withdraw into their shells to avoid conflicts. They give up their personal goals and relationships. They stay away from the issues over which the conflict is taking place and from the people they are in conflict with. Turtles believe it is hopeless to try to resolve conflicts. They feel helpless. They believe it is easier to withdraw (physically and psychologically) from a conflict than to face it.

2. *The Shark* (Forcing). Sharks try to overpower opponents by forcing them to accept their solution to the conflict. Their goals are highly important to them, and the relationship is of minor importance. They seek to achieve their goals at all costs. They are not concerned with the needs of other people. They do not care if other people like or accept them. Sharks assume that conflicts are settled by one person winning and one person losing. They want to be the winner. Winning gives sharks a sense of pride and achievement. Losing gives them a sense of weakness, inadequacy, and failure. They try to win by attacking, overpowering, overwhelming, and intimidating other people.

3. *The Teddy Bear* (Smoothing). To Teddy Bears, the relationship is of great importance, while their own goals are of little importance. Teddy Bears want to be accepted and liked by other people. They think that conflict should be avoided in favor of harmony and believe that conflicts cannot be discussed without damaging relationships. They are afraid that if the conflict continues, someone will get hurt, and that

would ruin the relationship. They give up their goals to preserve the relationship. Teddy Bears say, "I'll give up my goals, and let you have what you want, in order for you to like me." Teddy Bears try to smooth over the conflict in fear of harming the relationship.

4. *The Fox* (Compromising). Foxes are moderately concerned with their own goals and about their relationships with other people. Foxes seek a compromise. They give up part of their goals and persuade the other person in a conflict to give up part of his goals. They seek a solution to conflicts where both sides gain something— the middle ground between two extreme positions. They are willing to sacrifice part of their goals and relationships in order to find agreement for the common good.

5. *The Owl* (Confronting). Owls highly value their own goals and relationships. They view conflicts as problems to be solved and seek a solution that achieves both their own goals and the goals of the other person in the conflict. Owls see conflicts as improving relationships by reducing tension between two people. They try to begin a discussion that identifies the conflict as a problem. By seeking solutions that satisfy both themselves and the other person, owls maintain the relationship. Owls are not satisfied until a solution is found that achieves their own goals and the other person's goals. And they are not satisfied until the tensions and negative feelings have been fully resolved.

Choose the best answer to each question.

1. Two good friends have an argument. They decide to put aside their difference in order to keep their friendship. Both are managing the conflict like
   (1) turtles   (3) teddy bears
   (2) sharks   (4) owls

2. Someone who manages conflicts like an owl would probably make a good
   (1) spouse   (3) army sergeant
   (2) athlete   (4) lawyer

3. A worker suggests a new way of doing something. Her boss, who devised the current method, refuses to try the new method, saying simply that it will not work. The boss has managed the conflict like
   (1) an owl   (3) a fox
   (2) a shark   (4) a turtle

4. Someone who manages conflicts like a fox would probably make a good
   (1) manager   (3) director
   (2) athlete   (4) negotiator

Five Ways of Handling Conflict

Sam Leonard

How do individuals handle conflict? I have observed five methods people employ when encountering conflict in their everyday lives.

The first method is that of enforcement.

When I am in a conflict situation and I assume an enforcing mode, I want the rules followed. I expect the regulations to be carried out in every detail. I want to ensure that you do it my way.

The second mode for handling conflict is avoidance.

If I am in an avoiding mode, I seek to move away from the conflict. I need to get away from the fire as quickly as possible. Note that this is not the same as denial. In avoidance, I am aware of the conflict but make a conscious choice to avoid it.

The third mode for handling conflict is conciliation.

If I am in a conciliating mode, I will try to meet as many needs of the other party as possible. I will put my own needs aside or in second place in order to make peace.

The fourth mode for handling conflict is that of consensus building or collaboration.

In this mode, I want to identify as many needs and interests, including my own, that are operative in that conflict situation. Then I try to build a solution based on all of those needs. In consensus building, the best resolution will address as many of the needs of the persons present as possible.

The fifth way of handling conflict is that of bargaining or compromising.

When I am bargaining in a conflict situation, I start at point A, you start at point C, and we meet in the middle at point B. Compromising basically is incremental bargaining whereby we inch towards one another until a median is reached.

All of these are appropriate ways of handling conflict. Different situations call for different modes.

The *enforcing mode* is appropriate when the conflict has escalated to such a degree that it is out of hand. When the Ku Klux Klan and the Jewish marchers attempt to interface with each other, it is appropriate for security forces to move to keep peace and order, and to de-escalate the conflict. By enforcing a buffer zone, the safety of all is assured.

In a domestic violence episode when a woman is being beaten, this is not the time for consensus building. It is the time for avoidance. She needs to move away from that conflict situation as quickly as possible. Whenever safety issues are involved, *avoidance* is an appropriate way of dealing with conflict.

There are other conflict situations in which *conciliation* is important to use. It is Maurice and Josie's anniversary. Maurice strongly wants to go to a French restaurant. Josie has a taste for German cuisine. But Josie sees how important it is to Maurice that Josie go to the French restaurant. *The issue is not that important to Josie.* The relationship is more important than winning the argument. What does Josie do? She accommodates Maurice. Josie puts her need to have German food on hold because the other is so important to Maurice.

The most effective mode for handling conflict in a relationship is *collaboration*. These interconnections may be personal, professional, national or international. When relationships involve high stakes with long-term consequences, consensus building should be the preferred method.

Bargaining is appropriate when the stakes are low and the activity is fun. Usually a commodity is involved. A perfect example of bargaining in our culture is the ritual of buying a car. I visit the dealer, look at the sticker price, and see that it is inflated. Everybody in this culture knows the posted price is outrageous, including the salesperson. So I, as the buyer, enter the game of offering a ridiculously low figure for the car. We haggle back and forth until we agree on the price, generally somewhere in the middle.

Let us return to a more primitive mode of bargaining. It was a Friday night in the Old City of Jerusalem. A friend and I were shopping for Persian rugs. We went into shop after shop. At the time I knew nothing about Arab culture. Finally, I found three rugs I really wanted. The shopkeeper offered these rugs at an exorbitant price—$600. I told him I would pay $50. The game began. The negotiations continued for three hours over coffee. I finally bought the rugs for $200. When I returned to the States, the rugs were appraised at only $100. Such a deal! I was burned in this "bargain." (This was the same trip where my expert negotiation skills got me chased by another shop owner carrying a knife.)

Choose the best answer to each question.

5. Conciliation is a good way for husbands and wives to handle conflict when one of them
   (1) doesn't care too much about the particular issue they disagree on
   (2) will become violent
   (3) is always willing to put his or her needs aside for the other
   (4) wants to meet in the middle

6. Which way of handling conflict would probably lead to the best long-term solution of a dispute between workers and management?
   (1) enforcement
   (2) avoidance
   (3) conciliation
   (4) consensus building

7. Notice that each article describes five ways to handle conflict. The names are different, but the strategies are essentially alike. Match each name from "Conflict Strategies: What Are You Like?" with a similar strategy from "Five Ways of Handling Conflict."

   _____ 1. The Turtle (Withdrawing)   a. Enforcement
   _____ 2. The Shark (Forcing)   b. Avoidance
   _____ 3. The Teddy Bear (Smoothing)   c. Conciliation
   _____ 4. The Fox (Compromising)   d. Collaboration
   _____ 5. The Owl (Confronting)   e. Bargaining

The Writing Process

In Unit 3, you wrote three first drafts. Choose the piece that you would like to work with further. You will revise, edit, and make a final copy of this draft.

   _____ your problem/solution essay based on a neighbor dispute on page 96
   _____ your solution to a problem on page 108
   _____ your personal experience essay about an event that taught you a lesson on page 116

Find the first draft you chose. Then turn to page 176 in this book. Follow steps 3, 4, and 5 in the Writing Process to create a final draft.

As you revise, check your draft for these specific points:

Problem/solution essay: Make sure you included an introduction to the problem situation and a conclusion.

Solution to a problem: Check to see that you applied appropriate ideas from the reading selection.

Personal experience essay: Be sure you included your personal thoughts about what you learned from the experience and used at least one device to capture your readers' interest.

Unit 4 Attitudes toward Work

Attitude is how you feel and act toward things. It influences the way you see things. In this unit, you will explore different attitudes toward work. You will read about a man whose positive attitude helped him overcome prejudice and succeed in several ventures. You will read what one character in a play has to say about the value of work. And you will learn some valuable tips on how to improve your own attitude toward—and enjoyment of—work.

Before you begin Unit 4, think about your attitude. Does it help you toward your goals, or does it hold you back? What is your attitude toward work? Does it affect your work? If so, how?

▶ **Be an Active Reader**

As you read the selections in this unit
- Put a question mark (?) by things you do not understand.
- <u>Underline</u> words you do not know. Try to use context clues to figure them out.

After you read each selection in this unit
- Reread sections you marked with a question mark. If they still do not make sense, discuss them with a partner or your instructor.
- Look at words you <u>underlined</u>. Discuss any words you still don't understand with a partner or your instructor, or look them up in a dictionary.

Lesson 10 ▶ LEARNING GOALS

Strategy: Use your background knowledge
Reading: Read a biography
Skill: Understand chronological order
Writing: Write a biographical sketch

Before You Read

When you read the story of a real person's life, you are reading a **biography.** It is written by someone who investigated that person's life and possibly interviewed the person as well as family and friends. A biographical entry in an encyclopedia tells you basic facts of a person's life. But a biography in a book or a biographical article in a magazine tells you much more about the subject's life.

The biography "Brady Keys, Jr." was written by football star Rosey Grier for a book about people he admires. Before you read the biography, think about other biographies you have read. Below is a list of things you might expect to find in a biography.

- when and where the subject of the biography was born
- the subject's early childhood upbringing
- the main events of the subject's life
- anecdotes—short accounts of interesting events in the subject's life
- the subject's traits, both good and bad
- quotations from the subject
- quotations from the subject's friends and relatives
- the biographer's feelings about the subject

Preview the Reading

Read the title and the opening quotation. Think of what it tells you about the kind of man Brady Keys, Jr., is. Look at the photograph and read the caption for more details.

Set Your Strategy: Use Your Background Knowledge

You can use your **background knowledge**—what you already know—about biographies to help you understand and organize the information about Brady Keys, Jr. As you read the biography, look for the kind of information you can expect to find. Notice when the biographer is objective and when he is being subjective—expressing his feelings about Brady Keys, Jr. When you are finished reading the selection, you will have a chance to decide which elements of biographies were included in "Brady Keys, Jr."

All-American is a term applied to people who are the best in certain national sports. The author of the following biography was himself an all-American football player. He believes that Brady Keys, Jr., is all-American not only in sports but also in his attitude toward work, people, and life in general.

Brady Keys, Jr.

Rosey Grier

With me, you get a chance to make a real difference.
You get a chance to make a statement.
—Brady Keys, Jr.

Brady Keys, Jr., in front of one of his fast-food restaurants.

Brady Keys, Jr., grew up dirt poor during the 1940s, barely surviving with only his mother in Austin, Texas. They were too poor for new shoes, too poor for regular meals. About the only thing his mother could afford to give her son was dreams. And that she did. The day her eight-year-old boy came to her and told his mama he dreamed of becoming a professional football player and successful businessman, she didn't hesitate in her encouragement. "Yes," she replied. "Yes, you can. Yes, you will."

Recalling the memory, Keys said, "From that moment on, I was pointed in the direction of success."

Almost fifty years later Keys has lived a life of dreams come true—for himself and countless others he has befriended along the way. Brady Keys, Jr., did indeed become a star professional football player, as well as a self-made millionaire businessman with a Midas[1] touch for making money.

---

1. Midas (MY/dus) a king in Greek myths who had the power to turn everything he touched into gold

But the journey from little-boy dreams to adult success has been a long one for Keys, one filled with twists and turns, detours and dead ends. Looking back, Keys said, "The greatest personal obstacle in my career was my tremendous ability to get off track and chase women at a very young age. I just didn't feel that much else was important at a time when I had everything available to me."

As a teenager, Keys experienced the intoxicating attention that accompanies athletic stardom. He was blessed with a natural ability to handle a football, and made the varsity football team in both junior high and high school. When his mother married while he was still in high school and moved the family to Los Angeles, California, Keys got involved in other sports, too.

By the time his graduation rolled around, Keys had caught the attention of recruiters from several colleges. He even had an offer from a major league baseball club, the Brooklyn Dodgers.

In those days, he said, "they wouldn't let you play two sports." Forced to choose, Keys decided, "I didn't like baseball."

Keys had his eye on the future: he wanted to go to college. So he was drawn to an offer that included a scholarship from the University of California at Los Angeles. But his high school grades weren't scholarship material, and he ended up at a local junior college.

He discovered that his natural ability on the football field didn't apply to the classroom. His grades didn't cut it, so he dropped out of college and began playing semi-pro football.

A couple of years later, Keys got a second chance at a college education, when a scout from the Pittsburgh Steelers spotted him playing semi-pro ball and realized his potential. The scout promised to help Keys attend college until he could be legally drafted into the National Football League. During this time, he met and married Anna, who's been his wife ever since.

Keys entered Colorado State University. This time around, he knuckled down to his studies, working hard to get better grades. He also excelled at college football. By his third year, he qualified for the pros. "The Steelers sent me to CSU and then they pulled me out," Keys said.

For the next six years Keys played defensive halfback with the Steelers. He became an All-Pro on a Steelers defense that routinely finished first or second in its category.

His pro football dream realized, Keys turned his sights on his other ambition—to be a businessman. In 1967, with unprecedented financial backing from the Steelers, he started his first fast-food restaurant in San Diego, California. He christened it All-Pro Chicken.

Although things seemed to be going his way, Keys began having disagreements with Pittsburgh's management that led to his being traded to the Minnesota Vikings. He played for them for a year. Then, after a short stint with the St. Louis Cardinals, Keys left the NFL altogether—he said he is fairly certain he was being blackballed by team owners who were uncomfortable with his burgeoning[2] success as a business owner.

But Keys had no intention of becoming a quitter. Faced with a challenge, Keys always relied upon his religious faith to see him through: "God has just blessed me, and blessed me, and blessed me. And forgiven me, and put me on the right track," he said. "Each time I lose something, He gives me more than I had before."

Based on his own experiences, Keys encourages teens and young adults to "seek God for your answers and guidance."

With religion as his compass, Keys went full steam ahead into the business world. Back in San Diego, he ran his restaurant with the help of his mother-in-law, her two sons, and his wife. It was such a success that within three months, he opened a second restaurant in San Diego, and then a third in Pittsburgh. That restaurant became the cornerstone of his franchise. Suddenly, it seemed, All-Pro Chicken was popping up all across the country.

After several profitable years in business, Keys made another major move in 1970: he bought a Burger King in Detroit's inner city. Just as he had with All-Pro, Keys grew the business, buying and building more Burger Kings until he became one of the largest employers of young people in Michigan. He also became the first black in the country to become a major franchiser of fast-food restaurants.

Just as important, he developed a reputation for being one of the best, achieving an employee retention rate that became the envy of his industry. "I don't lose people," he said. "With me you get a chance to make a real difference. You get a chance to make a statement."

Bigger businesses recognized that Keys was powerful competition and wanted to cash in on his success. In 1971, he struck a deal with Kentucky Fried Chicken to merge his All-Pro chain with their business. In the early eighties, Kentucky Fried Chicken made him an offer that sent him to Albany, Georgia, where he now lives. "I just couldn't turn that one down," he said.

Today, restaurants are only a portion of Keys's business interests. Through a series of deals in 1990, he sold all his Burger Kings, and he's cut back to only eleven Kentucky Fried Chicken restaurants.

Success has been a mixed blessing for Keys, though. Between his football talent and his business acumen,[3] achieving wealth unusual for a black man in the sixties and seventies, Keys often has been thrust into public view. He's been criticized, scrutinized,[4] and ostracized[5] more times than he cares to remember during the past three decades.

---

2. burgeoning (BER/jun/ing) growing or developing rapidly
3. acumen (uh/KYOO/mun) sharpness and quickness in understanding
4. scrutinized (SKROO/tun/yzd) examined carefully
5. ostracized (OS/truh/syzd) shut out from a group; shunned

By many measures, Keys is a man of contrasts and contradictions. He defies stereotypes held by whites and blacks. A private man who believes a person should be measured by his deeds, he avoids confrontation, but he can't seem to escape controversy. He's regarded as a compassionate, generous man by those who know him personally; publicly, he's been subjected to considerable scrutiny—often tinged with racism—by people who question his motives and seem to watch his every move as he goes about his business.

"Being Brady Keys is very difficult in this town," he once told a reporter for *The Albany Herald.* "There's always a story going around about me. I'm extremely misunderstood."

Take the time he decided to buy a house in the suburbs. He struck a deal, never dreaming his new home included a bonus: a racial tug-of-war.

But in no time, townsfolk were talking. Rumor had it Keys was working on a plan to infiltrate[6]—and therefore integrate—the suburb's all-white country club. White business associates tried to talk him out of moving. Blacks in the community pushed him to put up a fight.

In the end, when his boxes were packed and moving trucks were backing into his new driveway, Keys was forced to face a hard truth: no matter whether he moved or stayed put, he'd made a lot of people angry.

"All I wanted was a house to live in," he said. "I really didn't want a fight."

But in one way or another, he's been battling discrimination most of his life.

For instance, some blacks in Arbor Hill, the "Little Harlem" part of his town, have faulted Keys for not using his power, money, and influence to fight against the city's undercurrent of racism. Other blacks, Keys said, assume that he's become too big "to relate to the little people."

White society, on the other hand, has seemed to accept him because of his wealth and business success. But the acceptance is tenuous[7] at best.

Keys recalled an incident from his early days in Albany. He was in his restaurant, doing some paperwork, when a white couple walked in. Spotting Keys at his desk, they called him an "uppity nigger," loudly enough for all to hear, suggesting that he had no business "sitting there acting like he owns something."

Keys has never been one to waste time or energy challenging his critics or defending his position. "I never strike back when people accuse me falsely," he said. Rather than confront the couple—and point out that he owned not only the very restaurant they were about to eat in, but several others—he decided it was time to work on his image. "I started portraying myself as a professional football player and sponsoring more community events."

---

6. infiltrate (in/FIL/trayt) enter an enemy's territory
7. tenuous (TEN/yoo/us) weak or slight

Still, racism has continued to haunt Keys.

In 1991, when he bought WJIZ-FM, a local radio station that happened to be both Albany's largest and only black station, the volume of rumors about him increased. Folks speculated that he wanted to control the media so he could become mayor. Some even considered him dangerous after he added editorials and talk shows to the station's regular format of music and news.

As mysterious as Keys's motives may at times seem to the general public, close friends and business associates describe him as a genuine and unusually generous man who goes out of his way to help people. It's ironic, they say, that Keys seems to invite speculation precisely because he avoids publicity for his good deeds.

John Draper, a long-time friend and business associate, described Keys as "very human. You need that in business, where people are often very cold," Draper said. "There are not too many successful entrepreneurs[8] like that. Black or white."

Draper believes Keys has succeeded because "he's like that motto for that California-brand wine: 'We sell no wine before its time.'"

"He does things the good, old-fashioned way," Draper said. "He's an American hero because he's *worked* at it."

Keys said, "The single most important quality that led to my success is my absolute perseverance.[9] I just will not give up, regardless of what it is. The second thing is focus."

Throughout his career, Keys has earned a reputation as a man who enjoys taking a chance on those who seem to have no chance at all. He's been known to hire people just out of jail or who have overcome drug addictions. A father of six, he loves children and takes particular delight in giving young people a head start and coaching them to success.

Take R. J. Watkins, for example. He was a high school dropout who wanted to be a radio and TV producer with his own business. But banks weren't exactly lining up to give him the money he needed to create his dream. Then he crossed paths with Keys.

"I'm successful today because of Brady Keys's help," said Watkins. "He's an angel to me."

Without Keys's financial backing, Watkins said, no bank was going to loan him money to start his business. That was more than a decade ago. Today, the Detroit, Michigan, production company that Keys helped him set up has several programs in syndication—on radio, TV, and video.

"I'm going to do everything in my power to keep this going as long as I live," Watkins said of his business. "I'd do anything not to let him down."

Watkins is part of a large and devoted following who can trace the

---

8. entrepreneurs (ON/truh/pruh/nerz) people who organize and run a business, trying to make a profit but taking the risk of a loss

9. perseverance (per/suh/VEER/uns) the trait of sticking to a purpose or a goal

turning points in their lives to Keys. Another is Brenda Ramsey, a former restaurant employee, who launched a chain of hair-styling salons with Keys's help. Starting in Detroit, she ambitiously expanded her business to other parts of the country, including Albany, with Keys's encouragement.

Ramsey said she thinks of Keys like a father. "He pushes you to see your own potential and then lets you do what you can do. He likes most to help people develop their own skills. But if you run into problems, you can always run back to him. You can call him anytime you need anything."

Though some may doubt Keys's motivations for gambling on unproven business risks, he is driven by a simple and sincere desire "to take care of the people who have helped me get where I am," he said. "I feel that's what God wants me to do."

"I'm not out to make a lot of business conquests," he added. "I turn down deals all the time."

Those who know him say that's not bragging, it's just the facts.

"You wouldn't think an ex–football player would be as unassuming as he is," said John Richards, a reporter for the Albany newspaper who's written about Keys. Even though Keys has been active in the community, setting up a TV program designed to keep kids away from drugs and sponsoring entertainment events for young people, he "doesn't toot his own horn," Richards added.

That's how Keys wants it. People "will see who I am through my deeds," he explained, "not by what I say."

▶ **Revisit Your Strategy: Use Your Background Knowledge**

Check off each thing you found out in the biography "Brady Keys, Jr."

_____ when and where Brady Keys, Jr., was born

_____ his early childhood upbringing

_____ the main events of his life

_____ anecdotes, or short accounts of interesting events in his life

_____ both his good and his bad traits

_____ quotations from Brady Keys, Jr.

_____ quotations from people who knew Keys

_____ when the author was being objective and when he was being subjective

Did looking for the elements you expected to find help you understand and organize the information in the biography?

After You Read

A. Comprehension Check

1. Keys's ambition as a young boy was to be
   (1) an owner of All-Pro Chicken
   (2) a generous man who helps others
   (3) a pro baseball player and a college graduate
   (4) a pro football player and a successful businessman

2. The two most important qualities that led to Keys's success were
   (1) being old-fashioned and not taking chances
   (2) staying focused and not giving up
   (3) being generous and making friends
   (4) chasing women and playing football well

3. Keys believes people should be measured by
   (1) what they do
   (2) what they say
   (3) their financial success
   (4) their athletic ability

4. Keys said he is driven by his desire to
   (1) take risks
   (2) be accepted by both blacks and whites
   (3) build a business empire
   (4) take care of people who helped him

5. From reading the biography, you can infer that Rosey Grier
   (1) didn't know Keys personally
   (2) worked for Keys
   (3) knew and admired Keys
   (4) was totally objective about Keys

6. In the sentence ". . . he was being *blackballed* by team owners who were uncomfortable with his burgeoning success . . ." *blackballed* means
   (1) fired   (3) ignored
   (2) kept out   (4) traded

B. Read between the Lines

Check each statement that Keys might have said.

   ✓ **1.** "I would have gotten a scholarship to college if I had worked harder in high school."

   ✓ **2.** "I studied harder at Colorado State University than in high school and junior college."

   3. "I was too busy with my All-Pro Chicken restaurants to play football well."

   4. "I make my employees feel important to the success of my business."

   5. "I want people to know about all the good deeds I've done."

C. Think beyond the Reading

Discuss these questions with a partner. Answer them in writing on separate paper if you wish.

1. If you were to interview Brady Keys, Jr., for a new biography, what three questions would you ask him? Why?

2. Do you think Rosey Grier was mostly objective or mostly subjective when he wrote about Brady Keys, Jr.? Do you think another biographer would have told the story of Keys's life in the same way? If not, how might the biography have been different?

Think About It: Understand Chronological Order

The events in this biography of Brady Keys, Jr., are not always presented in the order in which they happened. When a story goes back and forth in time, readers can use dates and other clues about time to figure out the **chronological order,** or the order in which things happen in time.

A. Look at Chronological Order

Reread the first five paragraphs of the biography, starting on page 125 with "Brady Keys, Jr., grew up . . ." and ending with "Keys got involved in other sports, too." As you read, watch for words and dates that give clues as to when each event in Keys's life happened.

The time line below uses chronological order to organize the biographical events mentioned in the first five paragraphs. Complete the time line with events from the paragraph on page 126 that begins "As a teenager, Keys experienced . . ."

1940s	Born in Austin, Texas. Poor childhood.
Age 8	Dreams of pro football and business success; mother encourages him, points him toward success.
Teenager	Makes junior high school varsity football team. _____ _____ _____ _____
Adulthood	Chased women at young age. Becomes star pro football player. Becomes self-made millionaire businessman.
1990s	Dreams have come true.

Between the time Keys made the junior high school team and the time he chased women, you may have added these events on the time line: *Makes high school varsity football team; Mother marries; Family moves to Los Angeles;* and *Plays other sports in Los Angeles.*

 Tip   When you aren't given an exact time for an event, you can often infer the time. For example, you could infer Brady Keys was a pro football player in the 1960s because he would have been in his 20s then.

B. Practice

1. Reread the six paragraphs beginning with "Keys had his eye on the future" on page 126 and ending with "He christened it All-Pro Chicken." Then fill in the time line.

1950s	Fails to get college scholarship Starts junior college _____ _____
1960s	Meets and marries Anna _____ _____ _____ _____
	Starts first fast-food restaurants

2. The following events from "Brady Keys, Jr." are not in chronological order. Write the letter for each event in the correct chronological order on the time line.

a. Buys Burger King in Detroit

b. Buys WJIZ-FM

c. Accepts Kentucky Fried Chicken offer, moves to Georgia

d. Merges All-Pro Chicken with Kentucky Fried Chicken

e. Leaves the NFL

f. Sells Burger Kings, cuts back Kentucky Fried Chicken restaurants

1960s	Opens first All-Pro Chicken _____
1970s	_____ _____
1980s	_____
1990s	_____ _____

▶ **Talk About It**

With a partner, make a list of obstacles Brady Keys, Jr., had to overcome to achieve his goals. Then list the personal qualities in his attitude toward work that helped him overcome those obstacles. Discuss whether a good attitude toward work could help most people overcome obstacles to achieve their goals.

Write About It: Write a Biographical Sketch

Rosey Grier, the author of "Brady Keys, Jr.," interviewed Keys to learn about his life and his attitude toward work. Now you will have a chance to interview someone and write a biographical sketch about that person's life and attitude toward work. First study the sample, which shows how to write a biographical sketch.

Study the Sample

Read the steps below to see what the writer considered as she developed her biographical sketch.

Step 1: Picking a Topic. The writer of the sample sketch chose an acquaintance, Jamee Krause, who started her own hot dog business to support her family after her husband died.

Step 2: Developing and Organizing the Biographical Sketch. The writer thought carefully and listed questions to ask during the interview. Then she numbered them in the order in which she would ask them:

1. How old were you when your husband died?
2. How long were you married?
3. When did you first open your business?
4. Did you always want to own your own business?
5. Would it have been easier to work for someone else?
6. Why did you choose a hot dog business?
7. Do you like hot dogs yourself?
8. Did anyone help you start your business?
9. Do you like your work?

Now read the writer's biographical sketch on the next page. Then it will be your turn.

Your Turn

A. Prewriting

Step 1: Think of someone you know who has worked hard toward a goal and whose attitude toward work you admire. Arrange an interview with your chosen subject.

Step 2: Make a list of at least seven questions to ask during your interview. Include questions about standard information found in biographical sketches and specific questions about your subject's life and work. Leave enough space after each question to take notes during the interview. You can also tape-record the interview and fill in more details later if you choose.

Hot Diggity Dogs!

"One hot dog with everything on it, a small fries, and a chocolate shake!" yells out a counter worker.

"That's the best hot dog you could order," says Jamee Krause at her Hot Diggity hot dog restaurant. At 45, Krause is the top dog, so to speak, for Hot Diggity. She's as hot dog crazy as the crowd of teenagers and office workers pouring into her restaurant for lunch. "I love hot dogs, and I love what I do," reflects Krause, "but none of this would have been possible without my supporters—my kids, family, friends, employees." Krause credits this group with giving her good business advice and doing everything from baby-sitting to filling in on the grill when the flu struck her last winter.

Born on the South Side of Chicago, Krause didn't grow up longing to open her own business. She didn't know the first thing about the restaurant business when her husband of 12 years was killed in an auto accident. With two school-age children to support, Krause took a part-time job as a short-order cook at a neighborhood hamburger stand. Customers would often ask for hot dogs. Her reply was, "This is a hamburger stand. We don't have hot dogs." Finally, she began to think about giving the customers what they wanted. Not afraid of hard work and determined to provide for her children, Krause took some correspondence courses and read everything she could find about the restaurant business and about hot dogs. She opened Hot Diggity five years ago, and business has been booming ever since.

Krause plans to sponsor after-school programs at the high school to thank the people who helped her. "Everyone's done so much for me all these years," she explains. "Now I'm in a position to return the favors."

B. Writing

On separate paper, write a biographical sketch from the information you learned during the interview.

Tip Group together the answers to questions that relate to one main idea. Then write about each group of answers in a separate paragraph. Make sure to write a topic sentence that makes the main idea clear.

▶ **Save your draft.** At the end of this unit, you will work with one of your drafts further.

Lesson 11

Strategy: Restate
Reading: Read a dramatic monologue
Skill: Interpret a monologue
Writing: Write a humorous monologue

Before You Read

The reading selection in this lesson is a **dramatic monologue,** a long speech by a character in a play. A dramatic monologue reveals the character's thoughts and feelings to other characters in the play as well as to the audience. In this monologue, a character named Aunt Dan tells a character named Lemon—and us—about her attitude toward work.

Are some people's jobs more important than others? Should people be treated differently depending on their jobs? Do people's attitudes toward their jobs affect their job performance? You will learn Aunt Dan's opinions on these and other issues from reading her dramatic monologue.

The monologue is supposed to sound natural—not like a politician giving a formal speech, but like one friend talking to another. Think now of how people talk. Listen to a conversation between two people you know. Do they use phrases like "I mean" and "y'know"? Note one or two other phrases people use when speaking informally.

When you read the monologue, read it as if a person were speaking it. Imagine yourself as the actor playing Aunt Dan on stage, and read the words as you would say them aloud.

Preview the Reading

Read the introduction and the lines under the playwright's name for information about when the play *Aunt Dan and Lemon* was first performed and where the action takes place. The name AUNT DAN marks the beginning of her monologue.

Set Your Strategy: Restate

When you **restate,** you put something you have read or heard into your own words. Restating is a good way to check that you understand what you are reading. As you read the monologue, stop every so often and try to restate what Aunt Dan has just said. When you are finished reading, you will have a chance to identify restatements of some of Aunt Dan's key ideas.

In this scene, Lemon is a sickly 11-year-old girl who appears to have no friends her own age. Aunt Dan—a young American teacher at Oxford University in England—is her parents' best friend. Aunt Dan has some unusual views and loves to express them. Luckily for her, Lemon loves to listen. Following are some of Aunt Dan's views about work and workers.

from Aunt Dan and Lemon

Wallace Shawn

Premiere: New York Shakespeare Festival, New York City, 1985
Publisher: Dramatists Play Service, Inc.
Setting: Lemon's London apartment and various flashbacks

AUNT DAN

Now Lemon, I have to tell you something very important about myself. And there aren't many things I'm sure of about myself, but this is something I can honestly say with absolute confidence, and it's something that I think is very important. It is that I *never*—no matter how annoyed or angry I may be—I *never, ever shout at a waiter.* And as a matter of fact, I never shout at a porter or a clerk in a bank or anybody else who is in a weaker position in society than me. Now this is very, very important. I will never even use a *tone of voice* with a person like that which I wouldn't use with you or your father or anyone else. You see, there are a lot of people today who will simply *shout* if they're angry at a waiter, but if they happen to be angry at some powerful person like their boss or a government official, well then they'll *very respectfully disagree.* Now to me that's a terrible thing, a horrible thing. First of all, because I think it's cowardly. But mainly because it shows that

these people don't recognize the value and importance of all those different jobs in society! They think a waiter is less *important* than a president. They look down on waiters! They don't admire what they do! They don't even notice whether someone is a good waiter or a bad waiter! They act as if we could sort of all afford to have no respect for waiters now, or secretaries, or maids, or building superintendents, because somehow we've reached a point where we can really just *do without* these people. Well, maybe there's some kind of a fantasy in these people's minds that we're already living in some society of the future in which these incredible robots are going to be doing all the work, and every actual citizen will be some kind of concert pianist or a sculptor or a president or something. But I mean, where are all these robots, actually? Have you ever seen one? Have they even been invented? Maybe they *will* be. But they're not here *now.* The way things are *now,* everybody just can't *be* a president. I mean—I mean, if there's no one around to cook the president's lunch, he's going to have to cook it himself. Do you know what I'm saying? But if no one has put any food in his kitchen, he's going to have to go out and buy it himself. And if no one is waiting in the shop to sell it, he's going to have to go out into the countryside and *grow* it himself, and, you know, that's going to be a full-time job. I mean, he's going to have to resign as president in order to grow that food. It's as simple as that. If every shop clerk or maid or farmer were to quit their job today and try to be a painter or a nuclear physicist, then within about two weeks *everyone* in society, even people who used to *be* painters or nuclear physicists, would be out in the woods foraging for berries and roots. Society would completely break down. Because regular work is not one tiny fraction less necessary today than it ever was. And yet we're in this crazy situation that people have gotten it into their heads that regular work is somehow unimportant—it's somehow worth nothing. So now almost everyone who isn't at *least* a Minister of Foreign Affairs feels that there's something wrong with what they do—they feel ashamed of it. Not only do they feel

that what they do has no value—they feel actually *humiliated* to be doing it, as if each one of them had been singled out for some kind of unfair, degrading punishment. Each one feels, I shouldn't be a laborer, I shouldn't be a clerk, I shouldn't be a minor official! I'm better than that! And the next thing is, they're saying, "Well, I'll show them all—I won't work, I'll do nothing, or I'll do *almost* nothing, and I'll do it badly." So what's going to happen? We're going to start seeing these embittered[1] typists typing up their documents incorrectly—and then passing them on to these embittered contractors, who will misinterpret them to these huge armies of embittered carpenters and embittered mechanics, and a year later or two years later, we're going to start seeing these ten-story buildings in every city collapsing to the ground, because each one of them is missing some crucial[2] screw in some crucial girder. Buildings will collapse. Planes will come crashing out of the sky. Babies will be poisoned by bad baby food. How can it happen any other way?

---

1. embittered made resentful and bitter
2. crucial (KROO/shul) very important; necessary

▶ **Revisit Your Strategy: Restate**
Read each of Aunt Dan's statements on the left. Match it with its restatement on the right.

_____ **1.** ". . .these people don't recognize the value and importance of all those different jobs in society! They think a waiter is less *important* than a president."

_____ **2.** ". . . people have gotten it into their heads that regular work is somehow unimportant—it's somehow worth nothing. So now almost everyone who isn't at *least* a Minister of Foreign Affairs feels that there's something wrong with what they do."

_____ **3.** "We're going to start seeing these embittered typists typing up their documents incorrectly—and then passing them on to these embittered contractors, who will misinterpret them to these huge armies of embittered carpenters and embittered mechanics."

a. People who resent their jobs will do their jobs poorly.

b. Some people don't realize that every job is needed and is therefore as important as every other job.

c. Other people think certain jobs are unimportant, so now the workers in those jobs think they are too.

After You Read

A. Comprehension Check

1. Aunt Dan says she does not shout at people in lesser positions because she
   (1) is afraid of them
   (2) knows their importance
   (3) hardly even notices them
   (4) is talking to a young girl

2. When Aunt Dan says, "Everybody just can't *be* a president," she means that
   (1) some people are not qualified
   (2) the president's job takes up 24 hours a day
   (3) other jobs need to be done too
   (4) people have to be elected president

3. Aunt Dan believes that unless workers are treated with respect they will
   (1) let robots do these jobs
   (2) revolt and destroy buildings and planes
   (3) become concert pianists or sculptors
   (4) do a poor job or quit working

4. What is the theme, or main message, of Aunt Dan's monologue?
   (1) the snobbery of some people
   (2) the hard work of a waiter
   (3) the breakdown of society
   (4) the importance of all work

5. In the sentence "people . . . would be out in the woods *foraging for* berries and roots," *foraging for* means
   (1) digging for
   (2) searching for
   (3) stealing
   (4) planting

6. The author used all the methods below to craft the monologue *except*
   (1) objective writing   (3) colorful language
   (2) humor   (4) exaggeration

B. Read between the Lines

Check each statement that Aunt Dan would agree with.

_____ 1. It's all right to shout at waiters if you shout at your boss as well.
_____ 2. A waiter's job is just as important as the president's job.
_____ 3. Society depends more on people who produce food than on artists.
_____ 4. If a worker is treated with respect, he or she will do the job well.
_____ 5. People judge the importance of a job by how much authority the worker has.
_____ 6. We should try to make robots that do all the regular work.
_____ 7. People in low-level jobs usually do their jobs badly.
_____ 8. People should be respected for how well they do their job, not what job they do.

C. Think beyond the Reading

Discuss these questions with a partner. Answer them in writing on separate paper if you wish.

1. Do you agree with Aunt Dan's belief that all work has value and all workers should be respected? Why or why not?
2. Do you think a conversation between Aunt Dan and Lemon would be as effective as this dramatic monologue in getting across the same message? Why or why not?

Think About It: Interpret a Monologue

In a **monologue,** a character is thinking aloud. The character may be pondering a dilemma, or problem. Perhaps the character is arguing with himself or herself or trying to convince someone else, as in Aunt Dan's monologue. A monologue will usually reveal the character's personality as well as his or her ideas. You can learn a lot about a character by **interpreting a monologue.**

A. Look at Interpreting a Monologue

The playwright used humor to get Aunt Dan's message across. To explain her points, Aunt Dan exaggerates. She makes up absurd, or ridiculous, situations. For example, reread the first two sentences of the monologue:

▶ Now Lemon, I have to tell you something very important about myself. And there aren't many things I'm sure of about myself, but this is something I can honestly say with absolute confidence, and it's something that I think is very important.

Were you expecting Aunt Dan to reveal an earthshaking secret about herself? Now reread the next sentence in the monologue:

▶ It is that I *never*—no matter how annoyed or angry I may be—I *never, ever shout at a waiter.*

Were you a little startled and amused at Aunt Dan's "very important" secret? If so, why do you think you were?

_____

You may have been startled and amused because you expected Aunt Dan to reveal something far more serious. Surprise is one of the elements of humor the author uses throughout the monologue.

When you interpret the monologue, ask yourself what character traits Aunt Dan reveals about herself. Consider how the monologue makes you feel. Notice how the author builds the monologue to its absurd conclusion.

Tip Since it is spoken by a single character, a monologue must be particularly interesting to hold the audience's attention. When you read a monologue, think about the techniques the playwright uses to hold your attention.

B. Practice

1. To interpret the monologue, look first at what it tells you about Aunt Dan. Check all the character traits you think the monologue reveals.

_____ **a.** concern for all people   _____ **e.** talkativeness

_____ **b.** wild imagination   _____ **f.** selfishness

_____ **c.** respect for others   _____ **g.** sense of the dramatic

_____ **d.** lack of caring   _____ **h.** tendency to exaggerate

2. Now look at four techniques Shawn used to create humor: surprise, exaggeration, vivid images, and dire predictions. Read these excerpts from the monologue and check the techniques used in each.

a. ▶ maybe there's some kind of a fantasy in these people's minds that we're already living in some society of the future in which these incredible robots are going to be doing all the work, and every actual citizen will be some kind of concert pianist or a sculptor or a president or something.

_____ surprise   _____ exaggeration   _____ vivid images   _____ dire predictions

b. ▶ if no one has put any food in his kitchen, he's going to have to go out and buy it himself. And if no one is waiting in the shop to sell it, he's going to have to go out into the countryside and _grow_ it himself, and, you know, that's going to be a full-time job. I mean, he's going to have to resign as president in order to grow that food.

_____ surprise   _____ exaggeration   _____ vivid images   _____ dire predictions

c. ▶ within about two weeks _everyone_ in society, even people who used to _be_ painters or nuclear physicists, would be out in the woods foraging for berries and roots. Society would completely break down.

_____ surprise   _____ exaggeration   _____ vivid images   _____ dire predictions

d. ▶ embittered contractors, who will misinterpret them to these huge armies of embittered carpenters and embittered mechanics, and a year later or two years later, we're going to start seeing these ten-story buildings in every city collapsing to the ground, because each one of them is missing some crucial screw in some crucial girder. Buildings will collapse. Planes will come crashing out of the sky. Babies will be poisoned by bad baby food. How can it happen any other way?

_____ surprise   _____ exaggeration   _____ vivid images   _____ dire predictions

▶ **Talk About It**

According to Aunt Dan, some jobs are considered more important than others. Do you think respect for workers and workers' self-esteem should be based on the kind of job they have or on the quality of work they do? Do you think people should do their best no matter what kind of job they have? Explain.

Write About It: Write a Humorous Monologue

Aunt Dan's monologue uses humor to point out what might happen if attitudes don't change toward people who do certain jobs. In this section, you will have a chance to write a humorous monologue of your own about what might happen if people don't change their attitude toward something. First study the sample, which shows how to write a humorous monologue.

Study the Sample

Read the steps below to see what the writer considered as she developed her humorous monologue.

Step 1: Picking a Topic. The writer of the sample monologue chose as her topic people who always complain.

Step 2: Developing and Organizing the Humorous Monologue. To organize her ideas, the writer made a work sheet. First she selected and named the character and decided on a setting. She described the situation and listed examples of how people act. Then she listed possible outcomes if people don't change their attitudes.

Topic: What will happen if complainers don't stop complaining

Character and setting: Jessie Johnson, 23 years old, is speaking to a small discussion group.

Situation: Some people complain about everything.

Examples:

They start off every day moaning and groaning.

They complain about commuting, the weather, their jobs, their spouses.

They complain when things don't change but never do anything to change them.

They complain when things do change.

What might happen:

Everyone might start complaining.

People would be more dissatisfied and whine even more.

People would stop doing a good job because no one would think they did a good job.

People would stop working, period.

Now read the writer's monologue on the next page. Then it will be your turn.

Your Turn

A. Prewriting

Step 1: Choose a topic of your own, or write about what could happen if people don't change their attitude about

- household chores
- paying attention
- following procedures
- being on time
- having a boring job
- wanting higher pay

Jessie's Complaint About Complainers!

JESSIE JOHNSON

Do you have complainers where you work? You know who I mean. The ones who drag their bodies into work every morning and immediately start moaning and groaning about the crazy drivers out there, or the weather being too hot or too cold, or the coffee that looks like mud, or the spouse who can't do anything right. When it comes to actual work, complainers don't quit—complaining, that is. If the boss announces a new procedure that will make everyone's job easier, these people complain that we were better off doing it the old way. And they were the first to complain when we did it the old way! And what happens when the boss asks for suggestions on how to improve things? Then the complainers complain about being asked for suggestions!

What if all workers came in to work every day with chips on their shoulders and complaints about everything and everybody? Everyone would be listening to each other's whining, which would make everyone even more dissatisfied and whiny than before. The next thing you know, people would start to wonder why they should do a good job when everyone complains about it anyway. People might just stop working altogether. All over the world, work would just stop. And so would paychecks. Now there's a scary thought!

Step 2: On separate paper, make a work sheet on which you describe the situation and give examples. Also explain what might happen if the situation doesn't change. Use your imagination and some of the methods for creating humor: surprise, exaggeration, vivid images, and dire predictions.

B. Writing

On separate paper, write a humorous monologue from the notes you made on your work sheet. Don't forget to add a title that will catch your reader's attention.

Tip Read your draft aloud to a friend for comments. It is hard to judge how humorous your own writing will be to someone else.

▶ **Save your draft.** At the end of this unit, you will work with one of your drafts further.

Lesson 12

Strategy: Set a purpose for reading
Reading: Read an informative article
Skill: Analyze problems and solutions
Writing: Write an informative handout

Before You Read

The article "Get into the Flow" focuses on a problem many people face every day—disliking their work. Before you read the article, think about the work you do on the job or at home. Then check all the factors below that complete this statement: I would enjoy my work more if _____.

_____ I didn't have to do the same thing over and over again
_____ people would stop interrupting me
_____ I could concentrate on my work
_____ I weren't so bored
_____ I could do what I am good at
_____ I liked my co-workers better
_____ I liked my boss better
_____ I didn't have to get so much done in one day
_____ I didn't feel so stressed out about everything
_____ I were my own boss

Preview the Reading

Read the introduction and then the title. Look at the illustrations. Try to get an idea of what you will be reading about.

Set Your Strategy: Set a Purpose for Reading

Skilled readers **set a purpose for reading.** They have some idea about what they want to get out of a selection before they start reading. By setting a purpose, a reader can watch for specific information. Think of what you learned about the content of the article from previewing it. Then think of what you would like to learn more about. Would you like to know how to be happier on the job? Would you like to learn who controls your happiness? Would you like to find out how to bring happiness within your reach? Write your purpose here.

Purpose: _I want to find out_ _____

Look for the answer to your question as you read. When you are finished reading, you will have a chance to note whether you found it.

Most people want to be happy, but they have a hard time finding joy in this hectic, stressful world of ours. Some studies suggest, however, that happiness is within each person's reach. Who do you think controls your happiness? Read on to find out.

Get into the Flow

Katherine Griffin

Joe Huggins lives in a little patch of paradise, but at first glance it might appear that he spends most of his days in a kind of floury purgatory.[1]

Joe, who's 44, works 12 hours a day, up to six days a week in the cramped, windowless baker's nook at Relia's Garden restaurant in western North Carolina.

Each day he turns out more than a hundred loaves of bread, 400 or so rolls, several batches of granola, plus dozens of cakes, pies, muffins, cobblers, and cookies. It's all for the benefit of people who work up an appetite kayaking, rafting, canoeing, biking, and hiking along the Nantahala River—all the things Joe rarely has time to do.

So on a Thursday morning at the crack of dawn, gearing up for one of the busiest weekends of the year, you might expect to catch Joe grumbling, or at least looking dour now and again. Instead, he's bursting with enthusiasm, one moment sliding bread into the oven, the next elbow-deep in a bowl of biscuit dough, then pantomiming his latest technique for slicing cinnamon rolls. "I pulled out some dental floss, tied it around the roll, and

poof! They came apart perfectly!" Under his blue baseball cap, the crinkles around his brown eyes deepen, his perpetual half-smile widens into a grin, and his eyebrows rise as if to say, "Hey! Can you beat that?"

In an age when managers and blue-collar and clerical workers all find themselves increasingly squeezed by the demands of their work, Joe Huggins is a rarity—a person who manages not only to survive, but thrive in a job that's stressful, unglamorous, and repetitive.

"I love coming to work," he says. "Sometimes the work has a rhythm to it, a music. There are all these little dance steps I do. I lose track of time."

What's with this guy? Psychologist Mihaly Csikszentmihalyi (pronounced *chick-sent-me-high*) of the University of Chicago, would say he's developed a talent for "flow." Over the past 30 years, Csikszentmihalyi and colleagues have interviewed more than 8,000 people around the world, seeking an answer to the elusive question, What makes people happy?

It sounds like pretty touchy-feely stuff. But Csikszentmihalyi has taken his research out of the

---

1. purgatory (PER/guh/tor/ee) a place of temporary suffering or punishment

realm of abstract[2] musings[3] and into the nitty-gritty of everyday life. In his studies, participants wear beepers that go off randomly throughout the day, prompting them to fill out detailed questionnaires describing what they're doing and whether they feel challenged, bored, or anxious.

The results have been remarkably consistent. Across cultures and vocations—from Italian farmers to American executives—people describe the same state of mind when they talk about their most enjoyable experiences. It's what Csikszentmihalyi has dubbed flow: complete absorption in the activity at hand, a deep sense of exhilaration and clarity[4] and a feeling that there is nothing else one would rather be doing. It's what a tennis player experiences when she's perfectly paired with her opponent, and both mind and body are stretched to their limits, fully absorbed in the game. Musicians feel it when suddenly they can no longer say whether they're playing the music or the music is playing them. Chess players get into flow when a game so holds their attention that they're astonished to look up and find that several hours have passed.

Creating flow, then, requires some work. Hardly anyone experiences it during passive activities like watching television. In fact, one of the best places to experience flow is *at* work. Csikszentmihalyi has found that even though most of us say we'd like to work less and spend more time in leisure, we actually report more positive experiences at work than during our free time. In one study, people reported being in flow 54 percent of the time while working, but only 18 percent of the time during nonworking activities like reading, having friends over, or eating out. At work, people tended to say they felt challenged, happy, creative, and strong; during their time off they were more likely to feel passive, dull, weak, and dissatisfied.

To be sure, some jobs are inherently[5] more conducive[6] to flow than others. Managers and supervisors, whose jobs generally have more variety and challenge than rank-and-file workers', reported being in flow 64 percent of the time at work. Assembly line workers experienced it only 47 percent of the time.

Still, Csikszentmihalyi argues that *anyone* can develop a knack for creating flow experiences on the job. "When I first did restaurant work I did just sit down and cry sometimes," Joe says. "Just the overload of it—all the rush-and-remember details. I'm really not a rush-and-remember kind of guy." But he was determined to find a way to manage the stresses of his job. "If you're not enjoying your work, you're not enjoying your life," he says. "For me, it's a constant test to see if I can find the happiness in it."

Those who are able to make their jobs enjoyable, Csikszentmihalyi says, are less likely to find work stressful—no matter how hectic it is. In one study of executives, he found that those who were in flow most often at work were less stressed out and took fewer sick days than did colleagues who had the same work load but couldn't get into flow. If Csikszentmihalyi is right, one way to cope with job stress may be to become more rather than less engaged with work.

To Joe Huggins, this strategy makes perfect sense. Csikszentmihalyi's research is news to him, but spending a day at his bakery is like getting a crash course in creating flow on the job. It's something Joe has learned himself over the years, by trial and error. He has his own thumbnail[7] description of what flow is all about: "Energy begets energy," he says. "The more you use, the more you have."

It's about six in the evening, and Joe's long stainless-steel baker's table is lightly dusted with flour. Butter, eggs, mixing bowls, and a whisk lie

---

2. abstract (ab/STRAKT) something that is not concrete, such as an idea or a quality
3. musings (MYOO/zings) thoughts; ideas
4. clarity (KLAR/uh/tee) clearness

5. inherently (in/HIR/ent/lee) naturally
6. conducive (kun/DOO/siv) favorable; helpful
7. thumbnail very short or small

scattered about. Joe has been on the job since 6:30 this morning and is trying to wind down. But everyone else is revving up for the evening rush, and the demands are coming thick and fast.

As Joe butters pans, the pastry brush clacking furiously, a harried waiter rushes back and slides a stack of dessert dishes onto the bakery table. "Joe, we need twelve more cobblers for the group upstairs."

No sooner has Joe finished spooning out the cherry cobbler than kitchen manager Daisy Serle stops by, looking perturbed. "Heather just dropped a whole chocolate pie—should we take it off the menu?"

"Oh no, we've got lots more in the walk-in," Joe says, slapping dough out on the counter, lopping off pieces to roll into loaves, his hands in constant motion. He looks up and laughs at a couple of kitchen workers munching on hunks of the broken pie. "I think that waitress was tripped," he says.

It's Joe's determination to enjoy himself in the midst of a thousand and one distractions that explains how he can handle the stresses of his job. "When things get crazy, he can hold it together," says gardener Debbie Brown. "People look to him to gain a sense of groundedness in the midst of whatever chaos is going on."

Whether you're washing dishes or balancing spreadsheets, Csikszentmihalyi says, staying

focused on the task you're involved in keeps you alert to subtle details that help you perceive familiar experiences in a new way. People who are easily distracted, he says, are cut off from the flow experience.

Research by psychologist Jean A. Hamilton, of Duke University, suggests that high-flow people like Joe may actually use their brains differently from people who rarely get into flow. When college students who said they hardly ever experienced flow were asked to concentrate on a series of flashes or tones, Hamilton found that they used more mental energy than their typical baseline level. But high-flow students actually used *less* mental energy than usual when asked to focus their attention.

There are no ten easy steps to becoming high-flow—it's more intuitive[8] than that. The best way to begin, Csikszentmihalyi says, is to identify the kinds of activities you get completely immersed in, then try to transfer that absorption into other areas. "The nice thing about the flow experience," he says, "is that once you begin to recognize it, it kind of grows by itself."

For many of us, the biggest obstacle to flow is simple self-consciousness. In Hamilton's research, students who were constantly worrying about how others perceived them—How am I doing? What do they think of me?—found it difficult to achieve flow. She and Csikszentmihalyi have discovered that people who learn to focus attention not on themselves, but on what's happening around them, can transform stress into an opportunity to learn.

Approaching your work more as a game than a job is another way to start creating flow. The key is to make your work challenging enough so you won't get bored, but not so challenging that you become anxious and stressed. Joe, for instance, is constantly inventing tricks to make his work more interesting. When the bakery work starts to feel repetitive, he reminds himself that no matter how many times he's baked bread or pie, if he looks

8. intuitive (in/TOO/uh/tiv) instinctive; natural

hard enough, he's likely to see something new: a way to keep the rhubarb pie juice from spilling inside the oven, a trick to cutting pieces of pie so the crusts don't crumble.

"There ought to be one day a week when you don't do anything the way you're used to," Joe says. "You discover things." For instance, when he noticed how easy it was to lose track of the number of ingredients he'd heaped into a mixing bowl, he began creating visual patterns to help him remember. Now, instead of dumping in each tablespoon of cinnamon one after the other, he arranges them in a circle on top of the batter. When he's created a flower with seven petals of cinnamon, he knows he's got the seven tablespoons he needs.

Joe's coworkers speak of him with a kind of awed puzzlement. "A lot of times we sit and speculate about what makes Joe the way he is," says cook Peter Julius. "He identifies himself with his work, almost the way an artist does: Whatever he's doing is his canvas."

It's early in the evening, and Joe has headed home, traveling what is surely one of the loveliest commutes in America: a mile-long hike along a section of the Appalachian Trail, far above the Nantahala River. The leaves on the birch trees are a luminous green, catching the last light slanting over the western ridge.

Like most of us, Joe doesn't get into flow as easily during his time off. Or so he says. At home, evidence of his ability to make the ordinary extraordinary is everywhere. He and his girlfriend, Patrice Price, share two small houses on an acre or so of cleared land. He's covered his trailer home with wood shingles so it looks like a cozy cabin. He's planted the trees that line the east edge of the property and built a wall with the rocks he dug out to plant the trees.

"Even when you're playing, you're usually working at something," he says. "There's enough out there to find interest and challenge in almost any situation you find yourself in."

No matter how mundane.[9] "Did I show you my bathtub?" Joe asks. Sure enough, under a big poplar tree, he's set up an old porcelain bathtub. He points out the small round hole just below the rim at the end of the tub. "If you look out through the hole, it's just like a telescope," he says. "You can see different views of the mountains. It really focuses your attention."

---

9. mundane (mun/DAYN) commonplace; ordinary

Revisit Your Strategy: Set a Purpose for Reading
Look back at the purpose for reading that you set on page 144. Did you find the information you were looking for? If so, summarize it here.

_____

_____

If you did not find the information you were looking for, did you find other information that interested you? Do you feel the need to read other articles to find the information you wanted? Where else might you find the information?

_____

_____

After You Read

A. Comprehension Check

1. Joe Huggins thrives in his stressful job because he
   (1) doesn't have much to do
   (2) lives in a little paradise
   (3) finds ways to make his work enjoyable
   (4) has a house and girlfriend to go home to

2. What is "flow"?
   (1) not letting little things upset you
   (2) working hard
   (3) looking for new ways to do things
   (4) being focused on and excited by what you're doing

3. Flow is most likely to be achieved by those who
   (1) supervise others
   (2) do monotonous work
   (3) read a lot
   (4) are with friends

4. Each of the following is a way to get into flow *except*
   (1) doing activities that completely absorb you
   (2) finding the best way to do something and sticking to it
   (3) focusing your attention on the task at hand
   (4) making a game of your work

5. In the sentence "Across cultures and *vocations*—from Italian farmers to American executives," *vocations* means
   (1) nations   (3) continents
   (2) occupations   (4) hobbies

6. Compared to people who seldom achieve flow, high-flow people
   (1) are generally more self-conscious
   (2) more often become anxious and stressed
   (3) use more mental energy
   (4) are better able to focus their attention

B. Read between the Lines

Check off each person described below who you could infer was in flow.

_____ 1. a secretary who can't believe how quickly the day has gone
_____ 2. a store clerk who keeps asking if he can take a break
_____ 3. a student who doodles in his notebook during class
_____ 4. a football coach who is thinking deeply of new plays
_____ 5. a manager who willingly handles many problems each day
_____ 6. a factory worker who keeps watching the clock

C. Think beyond the Reading

Discuss these questions with a partner. Answer them in writing on separate paper if you wish.

1. Choose one of the factors you checked in Before You Read on page 144. Based on the article, what can you do to overcome the obstacle that is preventing you from being in flow?

2. Reread the poem "Factory Work" on page 26. Do you think the speaker of that poem is able to create flow at work? Explain your answer.

Think About It: Analyze Problems and Solutions

You learned in Lesson 7 that a **problem** is something that needs to be fixed, and a **solution** is what fixes the problem. The article "Get into the Flow" describes a common problem and a general solution.

A. Look at Recognizing Problems and Solutions

To recognize the general problem and solution in the article, we can use the five-step problem-solving outline introduced in Lesson 7.

Step 1: State the problem: People are unhappy at work.

Step 2: Identify the cause: People have not learned how to get "in flow."

Step 3: Think of possible solutions:

Solution 1: People can grumble and gripe about their work.

Solution 2: People can look for another job.

Solution 3: People can learn to create flow experiences on the job.

Step 4: Evaluate the possible solutions:

Solution 1: People will continue to be unhappy.

Solution 2: There is no guarantee another job will make them happy.

Solution 3: Learning to create flow experiences can make the job enjoyable.
    Choose the best one: Solution 3

Step 5: Develop a plan to carry out the solution and follow it.

The article discusses several specific problems and suggests specific ways people can learn to create flow.

Reread this excerpt from the article and then list the two steps suggested for carrying out the solution.

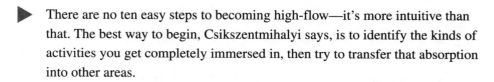

> There are no ten easy steps to becoming high-flow—it's more intuitive than that. The best way to begin, Csikszentmihalyi says, is to identify the kinds of activities you get completely immersed in, then try to transfer that absorption into other areas.

_____

_____

The first step is to identify the kinds of things you get absorbed in. The second step is to transfer that feeling into other areas.

Tip   When looking for good solutions to a problem in a reading selection, ask yourself, "What's the cause of the problem? Does the solution eliminate the cause?"

B. Practice

Reread these excerpts from "Get into the Flow." For each one, list the specific problem—why the people are not in the flow—and the plan for carrying out the solution "to create flow experiences." Some parts are done for you.

1. ▶ Whether you're washing dishes or balancing spreadsheets, Csikszentmihalyi says, staying focused on the task you're involved in keeps you alert to subtle details that help you perceive familiar experiences in a new way. People who are easily distracted, he says, are cut off from the flow experience.

   Problem: _People who are easily distracted are cut off from the flow experience._

   Plan: _____

   _____

2. ▶ Approaching your work more as a game than a job is another way to start creating flow. The key is to make your work challenging enough so you don't get bored, but not so challenging that you become anxious and stressed.

   Problem: _Both boredom and stress can keep you from achieving flow._

   Plan: _____

   _____

3. ▶ For many of us, the biggest obstacle to flow is simple self-consciousness. In Hamilton's research, students who were constantly worrying about how others perceived them—How am I doing? What do they think of me?—found it difficult to achieve flow. She and Csikszentmihalyi have discovered that people who learn to focus attention not on themselves, but on what's happening around them, can transform stress into an opportunity to learn.

   Problem: _____

   Plan: _____

   _____

   ▶ **Talk About It**
   Think about "flow" and its effects on people's attitudes toward work. With a small group, discuss whether you have ever had a flow experience in a job. List ways that group members might achieve flow in their jobs.

Write About It: Write an Informative Handout

The article "Get into the Flow" provides tips on how people can be happier at work by achieving flow. In this section, you will have a chance to write an informative handout that could help other people who do your kind of work to achieve flow. First study the sample, which shows how to write an informative handout.

Study the Sample

Read the steps below to see what the writer considered as he developed his informative handout.

Step 1: Picking a Topic. Suppose Joe Huggins were going to write a handout for his fellow workers. His topic would be "how to achieve flow in the kitchen."

Step 2: Developing and Organizing the Informative Handout. Joe would identify several specific causes for not being in flow and their solutions. He could organize his ideas as problems, causes, and solutions like this:

Problem 1: Easy to lose concentration
Cause: Work is repetitious.
Solution: Turn the work into a game by making visual patterns.

Problem 2: Bored because the work is monotonous
Cause: Work has become routine.
Solution: Look hard to find new way of doing something.

Now read Joe's informative handout on the next page. Then it will be your turn.

Your Turn

A. Prewriting

Step 1: Think of a type of work you have done during which you have sometimes been in flow. Choose one of the types of work listed below or one of your own.

- cleaning the house
- doing the dishes
- working in the yard
- doing a hobby
- factory work
- office work
- construction work
- painting the house

Step 2: On separate paper, identify at least two problems involving not being in flow, their causes, and their solutions.

Bakers, Get in the Flow

We all make almost overwhelming numbers of baked goods every day. We know the routine of our workday—day after day. Here are some suggestions for overcoming some common problems bakers face. What it takes is "getting into the flow" of that work.

Problem: *It's easy to lose concentration.*

Cause: Each day I turn out over 100 loaves of bread, 400 or so rolls, and dozens of cakes, pies, muffins, cobblers, and cookies. It all becomes a blur after a while, and I lose track of the number of ingredients I've added to the mixing bowls.

Solution: Try making a game of your work, such as creating a visual pattern. For instance, if the recipe calls for seven tablespoons of cinnamon, you might arrange the tablespoons in a circle on top of the batter. When you've created seven flower petals, you know you've got the seven tablespoons you need.

Problem: *I get bored because my work is monotonous.*

Cause: I bake the same goods day after day. The work has become routine.

Solution: Look for things in your routine that you never noticed before—for example, a way to keep the juice in a rhubarb pie from spilling inside the oven, or a method of cutting pieces of pie so the crusts don't crumble. Tricks like these will add a challenge to your work.

Remember, baking can be rewarding and enjoyable—that's why we became bakers. All it takes is getting in the flow.

B. Writing

On separate paper, write an informative handout describing the problems, causes, and solutions you listed.

Tip Make your handout easy to read and interesting to look at. For example, you can underline or highlight the headings *Problem* and *Solution* or make them **bold** if you are using a computer. You can also highlight each problem statement, as in the sample.

▶ **Save your draft.** At the end of this unit, you will work with one of your drafts further.

Writing Skills Mini-Lesson: More Subject-Verb Agreement

Verbs must agree with their subjects. Watch out for these special problems.

1. **Compound subjects.** Subjects joined by *and* are plural. A singular subject followed by such words as *plus, as well as,* and *along with* needs a singular verb.

         S   V

   Plural: **Leo and his brother are** both in computer sales.

         S   V

   Singular: **Leo** as well as his brother **sells** a lot of computers.

2. **Interrupting words.** Sometimes a phrase comes between the subject and the verb. To choose the correct verb form, look at the subject. Ignore the interrupting words.

       S   V

   Leo's **attitude** toward his duties **is** very positive.

3. **Inverted structure.** In an inverted sentence, the verb comes before the subject. Identify the subject and make the verb agree with it.

   - Many questions have an inverted structure:

       V   S   V   S

     What **are** Leo's **plans** for the future? **Does** his **supervisor** recognize his talent?

   - Sentences beginning with *Here* or *There* followed by a form of *to be* are inverted:

       V   S   V S

     There **are** many **opportunities** for advancement. Here **is** a **list** of training courses.

   - Sometimes when there is an introductory phrase, the sentence is inverted:

         V S   S

     Included in the training **are** a **course** on budgeting time **and one** on managing money.

Practice: Underline the subject of each sentence. On separate paper, copy the sentence, using the correct form of the verb in each blank.

1. (has, have) Leo's attitude toward his job _____ always been positive.
2. (has, have) How long _____ Leo and his brother worked at Electric City?
3. (wants, want) Leo plus two of his friends _____ to take management training.
4. (is, are) Here _____ the schedule and the material for the next training session.
5. (is, are) Included in the material _____ a manual for trainees.
6. (includes, include) Leo's plans for the future _____ a position in management.
7. (is, are) One of Leo's dreams _____ to own his own business.
8. (is, are) There _____ many people with a similar dream.

Reading Review

Getting Fired

Charles Grodin

I've been fired a number of times. The first time I was working as a car jockey for a Buick dealership in Pittsburgh. I was seventeen. My job was to move these new Buicks around in a big car warehouse. My problem was I had never driven a car that moved forward just by putting it in drive. A number of new Buicks didn't look so new after I had been there a few days. The boss called me over on a Wednesday and said he wouldn't be needing me on Thursday. I said, "So I should come in on Friday?" He said, "Not then either." Since I had never been fired, I didn't understand. "So I'll see you next week?" "No, we won't be needing you then either." I slowly got the message. It was a good lesson in cause and effect.

The next time I was fired I had a part-time job selling women's shoes in Miami, Florida, where I was going to college. I was an intensely preoccupied eighteen-year-old. I had a lot of things on my mind, and shoes weren't one of them. After not being able to find two or three shoes that customers had worn into the store, the manager called me over and said my performance was below shoe store standards. We shook hands, and I left before I put him out of business.

Next came my show business firings. The first time I was nineteen. At this point I was averaging one a year. Someone got the idea to give me a song to sing in a musical we were doing in summer stock. I still can't imagine why. After a couple of days someone else was singing my song.

My last firing, so far, came about fifteen years later. It was an Off-Broadway play. The original lead was fired, then replaced by another man, who was fired. Then they asked me to go in. I knew what had happened to the first two actors, but I was unemployed, so I went in. The show started to be received better, and the producer felt since the show was now better, they should get a star to play my part in order to help get them out of the red, which all these firings had put them into. The playwright's son said, "Gee, Dad, I wouldn't fire this Grodin guy. I'd keep *him*." The director, who was a famous actor, took over after they fired me; the show opened, got insufficient reviews to run, and closed. They said the star was miscast. Since the director-star was also a close friend of mine (I had actually recommended him for the directing job), this one ended a job and a friendship. This was the only time I disagreed with my firing.

A year later Neil Simon wrote a movie based on a story this same playwright had written, and much to the playwright's shock I was cast in the leading role. That was *The Heartbreak Kid*. Also, I wrote a play about someone getting fired that became a success.

I've always tried to learn from getting fired. I never spent much time on anger or resentment. I try to see where the firers are coming from. In the case of the play, the last one, the producer who fired me was coming from drugs.

Maybe the Great God of Firing thought I had some injustice coming to me for all those lost shoes, banged-up Buicks, and lousy singing.

I just read this piece over and realized I forgot two more times I was fired. Both were when I was working for *Candid Camera* about five years before my last firing. I think I forgot because just about everybody who worked for *Candid Camera* was fired. It was like part of the job. My final firing there came when Allen Funt asked me to put a door that wouldn't open on a men's room at JFK airport. I argued against the idea basically because people heading to a men's room after a flight aren't ideal candidates for a practical joke.

Mr. Funt insisted, and when we told these frustrated people they were on *Candid Camera*, their reactions were not amusing. Of course, it never made the air, and I was fired. Allen somehow blamed it all on me.

It's good to remember almost everyone gets fired in his lifetime. You are not alone. These firings can actually end up being funny stories you can tell—after several years.

Choose the best answer to each question.

1. Charles Grodin was fired from *Candid Camera* about five years
   (1) before being fired as a car jockey
   (2) before singing a song in a musical
   (3) before his part-time job as a shoe salesman
   (4) before playing the lead in an off-Broadway play

2. Each of the following problems caused Grodin to be fired from a job *except*
   (1) lack of skill in driving
   (2) lack of commitment to selling shoes
   (3) lack of singing talent
   (4) lack of acting ability

3. Which of the following is an example of exaggeration to achieve humor?
   (1) "The boss called me over on a Wednesday and said he wouldn't be needing me on Thursday."
   (2) "We shook hands, and I left before I put him out of business."
   (3) "I knew what had happened to the first two actors, but I was unemployed, so I went in."
   (4) "I try to see where the firers are coming from."

4. What solution does Grodin use for getting fired?
   (1) He gets angry and resentful.
   (2) He laughs at those who fired him.
   (3) He tries to learn from the experience.
   (4) He goes on to bigger and better things.

Bored at Work?
Take Charge of Your Lackluster Career!

Mark Golin, Mark Briklin, and David Diamond

Because we live in a country where many people are just as likely to salute large sums of money as they are the flag, it's tough sometimes to base your job satisfaction on factors other than cash, power, and prestige. But simply enjoying your job for what it is can provide you with a bigger payoff than the most overinflated salary or the biggest corner office. While that may sound just trite enough to be printed on one of those posters with seagulls flying around on it, think about this: You can sit around bemoaning that you are not in the fast lane, that you're underpaid, that the corporate world is not treating you the way you like . . . but it won't do you any good. Cash, power, and prestige must be given to you by someone else. On the other hand, self-esteem, pride in a job well-done, and a sense of importance are all bonuses you can give yourself. Unless you happen to be independently wealthy, you're going to have to put in forty hours a week whether you like it or not. So you've got nothing to lose and everything to gain by learning to find enjoyment in your work.

Give Yourself Permission to Like Your Job

Where did this notion that work is a trial which mortals must endure come from anyway? Why, when we're all free to make our own career choices, do we still end up resenting our job at some point or another? "There are two primary reasons I can think of right away," says Maynard Johnson, a psychologist and career counselor in New York City. "First, people resent that earning a living is wasting valuable time which they could spend enjoying themselves or uncovering what they suspect to be their true talents as a novelist or artist. If my clients raise this point, I usually ask them to recall their last long vacation. Was it two weeks of complete enjoyment? More likely, it was a week and a half of fun in the sun followed by a half week of 'If I watch one more sunset, I'm going to go out of my mind. Boy, I can't wait to get productive again.' "

If they don't admit to such vacation blues and their work dissatisfaction is serious, Johnson suggests that they take a three-month leave of absence if they possibly can. "I tell them to go work on their novel, enroll in a few classes, or just sit around watching TV, if that's what they want to do, and then come back to me in three months," he says. "By that point, most people will be frantic. They'll have lost track of the days, their self-esteem is at an all-time low, and they'll probably be irritable. While all work and no play is not good, all play and no work is disastrous. We need to feel that we are accomplishing something. And we also need some form of order in our life."

The second and perhaps more prevalent reason that people have a hard time liking their work is that they feel trapped. "Initially you have some choice in the kind of work you'd like to do." says Johnson. "But once you've been at a company for five years and have picked up a spouse, a mortgage, and a child, you have very little choice about jumping ship if things aren't turning out the way you planned. A steady paycheck can be the biggest manacle[1] of all. And while people never mind doing something of their own free will, they resent having to do it because they have no other choice."

If you have put in a number of years at a particular job and find that it just isn't satisfying you anymore, you may want to consider a career change. But if you simply find yourself resenting that you have to take what the company dishes out because you can't afford to quit, it may be time to prepare for yourself what Johnson humorously calls a cyanide capsule.

"It's a strange analogy," he says, "but if you ever watch secret-agent movies, they always have a cyanide capsule hidden somewhere on their body, in case they are captured. If the torture becomes too much to bear, they can simply swallow the capsule. In other words, they have an out. And having an out somehow gives them the strength to hold on a little longer in the hope that the situation may change."

Rather than packing cyanide, your out takes the form of an up-to-date résumé, a weekly glance through the Help Wanted section, and a sprinkling of visits to various industry functions where you can do low-key networking. This is not to suggest that you simply give up and get a new job. Rather, what you are doing is providing yourself with an alternative. Keep abreast of the job market, have your résumé at hand, and develop some connections so that *if* things get unbearable where you currently work, you *can* make a change quickly. The big payoff is that you will rid yourself of that constantly recurring resentment at being tied to your current position. Then, when things

---

1. manacle (MAN/ah/kul) a handcuff

get a little bothersome at the office, you can secretly smile and relax, knowing that you can split any time you want to.

How to Have a Positive Attitude Even When You Don't Feel Like It

While understanding that you aren't trapped and you aren't wasting your time can take you partway down the road to a better work attitude, there are a few more things you can do to perk yourself up on a day-to-day basis.

Career-management consultant and author Richard Germann estimates that four out of five workers dislike something major about their jobs. The trouble is, liking your job is essential for success. "Those who don't value what they do will never be successful at it," he explains. "Those who don't enjoy their work will ultimately fail."

At the core of adopting a positive attitude is accepting the simple notion that you must assume responsibility for your own situation. That's not to say that it's all your own fault if you seem stuck in a dead-end job. But you have more power than you realize.

It's largely up to you to do what you can to initiate a change in attitude. Here are some ways to get started:

• **Dream a little . . . plan a lot.** Germann often instructs his clients who are unhappy about their current job to fantasize about their dream job. It's fun, and it gets people to focus on their workplace ideals: everything from what they would really like to be doing every day to what sort of office environment they prefer. The point is to encourage folks to create their own definition of job satisfaction.

"I ask clients to start breaking down their ultimate fantasy into the smallest possible parts," says Johnson. "If a client sees herself as a junior executive working for a powerful boss in the marketing department when in fact she is currently a clerk working under a tyrant in purchasing, then we start looking for little stepping-stone goals that will get her from one position to the other."

Developing and following your own plan of action is one of the best ways to improve your attitude.

• **Think of yourself as autonomous.** In effect, this is a little mental trick that you can play on yourself. Start thinking of yourself as a small business or an independent contractor with one major client: your employer. Then allocate your time so that you not only meet the demands of your customers but also have room to develop certain aspects of your business that *you* (not the company) see as necessary for your future growth.

• **Separate work and play.** "Some people find themselves working the occasional extra hour or two in the evening," Johnson continues. "Then they start taking work home regularly to look at after dinner. Most people don't even notice it's happening, but suddenly they don't have a life apart from work, and they resent it."

Johnson is not saying that taking work home is taboo, but doing it *all* the time is.

"The interesting thing is that many people take work home, poke at it a little, and then go watch television. They never actually get any substantial work *done,* but on the other hand, they don't enjoy their leisure time, because that work is sitting there, tugging at their conscience. This wouldn't be so bad, except that if you always have some work lying around, you'll never enjoy yourself during your leisure time and you'll resent your job for putting you in the predicament you're in."

If you do have a heavy work load, Johnson suggests alternating evenings of intensive work with evenings of intensive leisure. "On Monday, Wednesday, and Friday evenings (or whenever appeals to you), do your work and try not to get sidetracked. But on your leisure nights, don't even bother taking work home if you can possibly help it. If you leave it at work, it can hardly sit on the coffee table, spoiling your evening with silent reprimands."

• **Strive for success outside of work.** This one is fast and simple: Take your hobbies and leisure activities as seriously as you do your work. This doesn't mean that you should drive yourself crazy over them, but at least strive for the same kind of proficiency and take the same kind of pride in them that you do in your work.

"This way, you can wean yourself from the feeling that work is the only thing that matters," says Johnson. "A trap many people fall into is that they get their whole sense of identity from the office. This may be great when things are going well, but things don't always go well. If your self-esteem is a direct outcome of your work situation, you're bound to have a bad attitude when the going gets rough. But if you can tie your self-esteem to outside interests too, then you can maintain a positive attitude even if the office forecast calls for a stormy week ahead."

Choose the best answer to each question.

5. Who can you infer has the most power to make a worker happy at work?
   (1) the company
   (2) the worker's boss
   (3) the worker
   (4) co-workers

6. Each of the following is a suggested solution to disliking your job *except*
   (1) defining the job of your dreams
   (2) bringing work home so that you identify more with your work
   (3) thinking of yourself as something separate from the company for which you work
   (4) doing something outside of work in which you can be a success

7. Creating a "cyanide capsule" by updating your resume, networking, and checking the want ads is a solution to which problem?
   (1) thinking how much you dislike your job
   (2) letting your job-search skills get rusty
   (3) being in a dead-end job
   (4) resenting your job because you don't have an out

8. Compared to Katherine Griffin, who wrote "Get into the Flow," the authors of this article
   (1) agree with Griffin on most points
   (2) agree with Griffin on only a few points
   (3) disagree with Griffin on most points
   (4) disagree with Griffin on all points

The Writing Process

In Unit 4, you wrote three first drafts. Choose the piece that you would like to work with further. You will revise, edit, and make a final copy of this draft.

_____ your biographical sketch on page 134
_____ your humorous monologue on page 142
_____ your informative handout on page 152

Find the first draft you chose. Then turn to page 176 in this book. Follow steps 3, 4, and 5 in the Writing Process to create a final draft.

As you revise, check your draft for these specific points:

Biographical sketch: Be sure you divided your sketch into meaningful paragraphs—each about one main idea and including the most interesting answers about that idea.

Humorous monologue: Make sure the reader will understand the humor you use. See if making your monologue more humorous and exaggerated will help get your point across.

Informative handout: Be sure you offer a specific solution to each problem and make your handout interesting by highlighting key information in some way.

Skills Review

This review will let you see how well you can use the skills taught in this book. When you've finished Units 1–4, do this review. Then share your work with your instructor.

Reading Skills Review

Read each selection and answer the questions that follow.

Mamon Powers Jr.

Personal Stats: 47, married, one daughter, 18, and a son, 15

Current Position: President, Powers & Sons Construction Co., Gary, Ind.

Education: B.S. Civil Engineering, Purdue '70

Reflections: Mamon Powers Jr. began working in his father's construction company when he was 11 years old. The lifestyle—being his own boss, running his own ship—was appealing. But his access to it was perhaps too easy for a kid who relished a challenge.

So it was that at 15, Powers spotted his goal after learning that there were no registered black professional engineers in the entire state of Indiana. "I wanted to be the first," Powers says. By the time he graduated form Purdue, then regarded as the nation's engineering mecca, someone else had grabbed that distinction. But Powers felt no less fulfilled. Purdue was no cakewalk for anyone, but for black students—who totaled 130 out of 26,000—the sense of isolation made it tougher.

After a brief stint with Amoco Oil Co. (which offered all engineers deferments from the Vietnam War), Powers rejoined his father in the family business, gradually taking it over and building it to the point where, in 1988, Powers Construction premiered among the B.E. INDUSTRIAL/SERVICE 100.

Even though they were well known and respected in the community, financial and entrepreneurial success did not translate into full social acceptance for the Powers family. The most striking evidence of this came in the mid-'80s, when Mamon applied for membership at a country club where several of the local contractor organizations—to which he and his father belonged—held regular meetings.

"I called around to my so-called friends to seek sponsorship," he recounts. "One guy said, 'Well, I'm about to quit,' another said, 'The food's horrible,' another never called back. Then I called our banker. He said, 'No problem, and, by the way, do you know there are no other black members there? If you were white, they would've been after you years ago.' He called back a week later, shaken. He said he didn't know me that well and, therefore, couldn't sponsor me."

Powers countered by calling the newspapers and threatening to sue. He also filed a complaint with the Indiana Civil Rights Commission. Finally, after a lengthy public battle with not one, but two clubs, he was offered and accepted a membership at the Woodmar Country Club. Since 1990, he and his family have been swimming and golfing at the club without incident.

"As I've gotten older, I've realized the world is just not as fair as I'd hoped," Powers sighs. "But the country club incident in particular really left a scar. It let me know that racism is still very much alive and well. On the other hand, in order for us to be effective and productive as a company, we can't let racism become a part of our thought process. If we do, it will hamper us. I tell everyone here, we have to be better than everyone else all the time. And in those fleeting moments when the playing field is level, we come shining through like stars."

1. Which statement from the article is an example of subjective writing?
   (1) . . . at 15, Powers spotted his goal. . . .
   (2) Powers rejoined his father in the family business.
   (3) "I called around to my so-called friends."
   (4) Powers countered by . . . threatening to sue.

2. When did Powers rejoin his father's construction company?
   (1) when he was 11 years old
   (2) right after his college graduation
   (3) after a brief job with an oil company
   (4) after he was accepted by the country club

3. Powers solved his problem of not being accepted as a member of a country club by
   (1) fighting legally for his civil rights
   (2) persuading his friends to sponsor him
   (3) proving that his business was a success
   (4) biding his time until the membership committee changed its vote

4. Powers's character can best be described as
   (1) hard-working and ambitious
   (2) lucky and carefree
   (3) demanding and never satisfied
   (4) talented yet spoiled

Progress toward Self-Sufficiency

The graph that follows summarizes data for a group of former welfare recipients over a three-year period.

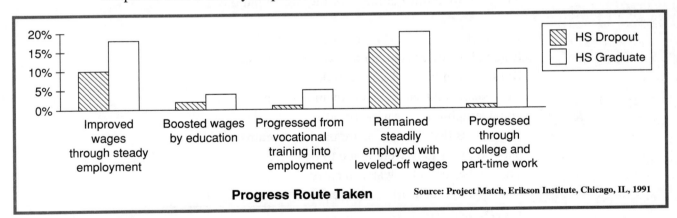

Source: Project Match, Erikson Institute, Chicago, IL, 1991

5. How did high school graduates and dropouts compare in their progress away from welfare?
   (1) Graduates earned triple what droputs did.
   (2) Both groups stood the best chance if they had vocational training.
   (3) Graduates were much more likely to make steady progress by any route taken.
   (4) Dropouts were just as likely to move away from welfare as graduates.

6. From the percentages of progress shown on the graph, you can infer that getting off welfare
   (1) is fairly easy if the right route is taken
   (2) cannot be measured
   (3) depends on a participant's desire to be self-sufficient
   (4) is more likely if you have steady employment

To be of use

Marge Piercy

The people I love the best
jump into work head first
without dallying in the shallows
and swim off with sure strokes almost out of sight.
They seem to become natives of that element,
the black sleek heads of seals
bouncing like half-submerged balls.

I love people who harness themselves, an ox to a heavy cart,
who pull like water buffalo, with massive patience,
who strain in the mud and the muck to move things forward,
who do what has to be done, again and again.

I want to be with people who submerge
in the task, who go into the fields to harvest
and work in a row and pass the bags along,
who are not parlor generals and field deserters
but move in a common rhythm
when the food must come in or the fire be put out.

The work of the world is common as mud.
Botched, it smears the hands, crumbles to dust.
But the thing worth doing well done
has a shape that satisfies, clean and evident.
Greek amphoras[1] for wine or oil,
Hopi vases that held corn, are put in museums
but you know they were made to be used.
The pitcher cries for water to carry
and a person for work that is real.

---

1. **amphoras** (AM/fe/rahz) ancient jars or vases

7. According to the speaker, how is a person like a pitcher?
   (1) Both need water.
   (2) Both want to be of use.
   (3) Both can be broken.
   (4) Both will one day crumble into dust.

8. The mood of the poem may be described as
   (1) exhausted
   (2) frustrated
   (3) passionate
   (4) lighthearted

Facts About Religious Discrimination

U.S. Equal Opportunity Commission

Title VII of the Civil Rights Act of 1964 prohibits employers from discriminating against individuals because of their religion in hiring, firing, and other terms and conditions of employment. The Act also requires employers to reasonably accommodate the religious practices of an employee or prospective employee, unless to do so would create an undue hardship upon the employer. Flexible scheduling, voluntary substitutions or swaps, job reassignments and lateral transfers are examples of accommodating an employee's religious beliefs.

Employers cannot
- schedule examinations or other selection activities in conflict with a current or prospective employee's religious needs,
- inquire about an applicant's future availability at certain times,
- maintain a restrictive dress code, or
- refuse to allow observance of a Sabbath or religious holiday,

unless the employer can prove that not doing so would cause an undue hardship.

An employer can claim undue hardship when accommodating an employee's religious practices if allowing such practices requires more than ordinary administrative costs. Undue hardship also may be shown if changing a bona fide seniority system to accommodate one employee's religious practices denies another employee the job or shift preference guaranteed by the seniority system.

An employee whose religious practices prohibit payment of union dues to a labor organization cannot be required to pay the dues, but may pay an equal sum to a charitable organization.

Mandatory "new age" training programs, designed to improve employee motivation, cooperation or productivity through meditation, yoga, biofeedback or other practices, may conflict with the non-discriminatory provisions of Title VII. Employers must accommodate any employee who gives notice that these programs conflict with the employee's religious beliefs, whether or not the employer believes there is a religious basis for the employee's objection.

9. You can infer that the right of an employee to have his or her religious practice accommodated by an employer ends when
   (1) accommodation involves any expense on the part of the employer
   (2) accommodation violates another employee's civil rights
   (3) a seniority system exists in the company
   (4) employees' work and vacation schedules have already been set

10. Suppose you have told your employer that the meditation in a mandatory training program conflicts with your religious beliefs. Your employer can require you to attend the training if
    (1) your employer excuses you from the meditation part of the program
    (2) you want to keep your job with the company
    (3) everyone else in your department attends it
    (4) your employer has already paid for your attendance at the program

Write About It

On separate paper, write about the topic below. Then use the Revising Checklist to revise your draft.

Topic: Think about a problem you once had at home or on the job—involving something at work or a dispute with another person. How was the problem solved? Could it have been resolved better? If so, how? Write a problem/solution essay.

Revising Checklist

Revise your draft. Check that your draft

_____ clearly states the problem, its cause, and the solution

_____ includes details about the problem and solution

_____ includes an evaluation of the solution

_____ includes a better solution, if appropriate

_____ contains an introduction and a conclusion

Skills Review Answers

Reading Skills Review

1. (3)	3. (1)	5. (3)	7. (2)	9. (2)
2. (3)	4. (1)	6. (4)	8. (3)	10. (1)

Write About It

Make changes on your first draft to improve your writing. Then recopy your draft and share it with your instructor.

Evaluation Chart

Check your Skills Review answers. Then, on the chart below, circle the number of any answer you missed. You may need to review the lessons indicated next to that question number.

Question	Skill	Lessons
1	recognize objective and subjective writing	6
2	understand chronological order	10
3	analyze problems and solutions	7, 12
4	understand characterization	1
5	compare and contrast	3
6	make inferences	4
7	compare and contrast, analyze writer's craft	3, 9
8	identify mood	2
9	make inferences	4
10	apply information	5, 8

Answer Key

Unit 1: The Working Experience

▼ Lesson 1

Revisit Your Strategy (p. 18)

Possible answers:

1. uncertain, tense, torn
2. disbelieving, disheartened, disgusted, angry

After You Read (p. 19)

A.
1. (2)   4. (1)
2. (2)   5. (3)
3. (4)   6. (4)

B. You should have checked 2, 3, and 5.

Think About It

B. Practice (p. 21)

1.

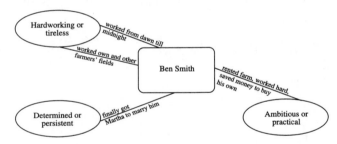

2.

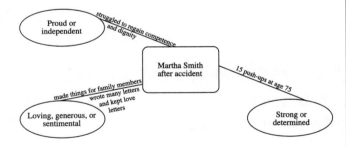

▼ Lesson 2

Revisit Your Strategy (p. 27)

Possible answers:

A.
1. fluorescent strips flared, ears grew numb, machinery
2. fatigue, wake at four, a dislocation of hours, always at an ebb.
3. Answers will vary.

B.
1. all day I stand, hot glue machine, not too close to the wheel that brings up the glue, metal shanks, shoe bottoms.
2. Answers will vary.

After You Read (p. 28)

A.
1. (1)   5. (3)
2. (4)   6. (2)
3. (2)   7. (3)
4. (3)

B. The following statements should be checked: 1, 3, 4, 6.

Think About It

B. Practice (p. 30)

1a. Possible answers include factory, flared all night, ears grew numb, machinery.

b. You might have felt tiredness, dullness, harshness.

2a. Possible answers include to cooling beds, undressing fatigue, wake at four, teeth soft as fur, dislocation of hours, inside-out, waking when the day is over, always at an ebb, unlike others.

b. You might have felt frustration, depression, loneliness, isolation.

3a. Possible answers include all day I stand, hot-glue, not too close, lasts weigh, big arms, he knows I hit him, had long hair before the glue machine got it, ate up my shirt, tried to get out, wheel spinning, someone with a brain, it's not bad here, people leave you alone, don't ask what you're thinking.

b. You may have felt competence, strength, lurking danger, touches of humor.

4a. Possible answers include grandpa's soul, the way the eggs fell, and the lamp broke like someone was trying to communicate to me, and he just dead this week, late October, lay some people off, I beat them all, all the moves on automatic, don't need to look at what I'm doing, leaves turn red when the cold gets near them, wading in red leaves, air snaps, tree-knuckles, see your breath rise, like your own ghost.

b. You might have felt confidence, acceptance, a positive attitude. Or you may have felt frustration, sadness, a negative attitude.

▼ Lesson 3
Revisit Your Strategy (pp. 35–36)

A. You should have checked statement 4. It gives the general information about what happened in the U.S. workforce between 1900 and 1994. It tells the trend—the way the data changed over the years. The first three statements are true, but they do not tell the general trend. They are simply statements of data.

B. You should have checked statement 3. Statement 1 is supported by the bottom line of the graph, which rises sharply from 1900 to 1960. Statement 2 is supported by the top line in the graph, which slants downward as it moves across the years. Statement 4 is simply data about one year on the graph. Only Statement 3 summarizes the trend in men's and women's employment from 1900 to 1994.

After You Read (p. 37)

A. 1. (3)   4. (1)
2. (4)   5. (2)
3. (4)

B. You should have checked statements 1, 2, and 5.

Think About It
B. Practice (p. 39)

1. Sample answer:

What does the graph show?	Compare: Look for similarities	Contrast: Look for differences
average salaries of men and women in selected occupations in 1996	most workers shown earned less than $40,000 in 1996	men's salaries are higher in 1996 in all but one occupation shown
average salaries of financial managers in 1996	second highest salaries shown for both men and women	average salary of men is significantly higher
average salaries of university information systems chiefs in 1996	highest paid of occupations shown in 1996	average salary of women is slightly higher than men's
average salaries of retail salespersons in 1996	lowest paid of occupations shown	average salary of men is higher than women's

2. Sample answer: In 1996, the average salaries of men were consistently higher than those of women in all but one of the selected occupations.

▼ Writing Skills Mini-Lesson: Commonly Confused Words (p. 42)

1. **Who's** the hardest-working person you know?
2. **There** are different kinds of work: paid and unpaid.
3. A homemaker and a factory worker both work, but **whose** job is harder?
4. **They're** both hard jobs with **their** own demands.
5. When you take care of **your** children, **you're** working hard.
6. If you work in a factory, **you're** also working hard, but **you're** earning money.
7. **It's** different for homemakers.
8. A well-run home and a happy family are **their** rewards.

▼ Unit 1 Review (p. 43)

1. (3)
2. (4)
3. (2)
4. (3)
5. (1)
6. (3)
7. (4)
8. (2)

Unit 2: Breaking New Ground

▼ Lesson 4
Revisit Your Strategy (p. 54)

1. (3)
2. (1)
3. (4)
4. (2)
5. (2)
6. (1)

After You Read (p. 54)

A. 1. (4)   4. (4)
2. (3)   5. (2)
3. (1)   6. (3)

B. The following statements should be checked: 1, 2, 5, and 6.

Think About It
B. Practice (p. 57)

1. a: he'd been with the president on several occasions

   c: he was "on guard," monitoring, careful

2. b: he had missed a lot of his son's games

   d: blurted out, words seemed to accuse him, lowered head, barely audible voice

▼ Lesson 5

Revisit Your Strategy (p. 64)
Possible answers:

1. handicapped bathroom facilities, wheelchair ramps, Braille numbers in elevators
2. firing, not promoting, giving bad reviews, reducing benefits, assigning jobs that a worker can't perform

After You Read (p. 65)
A. 1. (3)
   2. (4)
   3. (1)
   4. (2)
   5. (3)
   6. (4)

B. The following statements should be checked: 1, 3, 4, and 5.

Think About It
B. Practice (p. 67)

1. The following statements should be checked: a and b.
2. Sample answer: Yes. You are qualified for the job, and you have a significant disability. Since your boss considered you the best candidate, if you don't get the job it's probably because of your disability.
3. Sample answer: Yes. The boss believes she can do the job. An amplifier is not too expensive or too difficult an accommodation to make.

▼ Lesson 6

Revisit Your Strategy (p. 76)
Answers will vary.

After You Read (p. 77)
A. 1. (3)   4. (4)
   2. (2)   5. (3)
   3. (4)   6. (1)

B. The following statements should be checked: 1, 3, and 5.

Think About It
B. Practice (p. 79)

1. thought his work partner was the glowing exception to general female helplessness; hungrily listening to; endlessly repeated, and embroidered.
2. "malign neglect"; refused to recognize we'd arrived; felt awful and looked worse.
3. misery; unresponsive; a company union; indifferent; elaborate runaround; probably because no one knew, and no one wanted to take the trouble to find out.
4. Here is a sample answer: Management did not make any changes to accommodate women on the job. They treated women as they did men. We wore uniforms designed for men, which meant they did not fit correctly.

▼ Writing Skills Mini-Lesson: Pronoun Agreement (p. 82)
Sample answers. There may be other ways to fix some sentences.

To help in **Anita's** job search, **all** of **her** friends shared their ideas about job hunting with her. Then **she** and her friends made a list of places with job openings. I met Anita when **she** and a friend came to my office to apply for a job. After **Anita** and I had talked for a while, I knew she would be a good receptionist. While she filled out an application, I talked with my boss. **He** and I discussed her qualifications and agreed Anita's wheelchair would not be a problem. Then **he** and **I** offered Anita the receptionist's job. She was so excited she thanked the boss and **me** over and over. And she has been a big help to **him** and **me** ever since.

▼ Unit 2 Review (p. 83)

1. (4)   5. (4)
2. (3)   6. (4)
3. (2)   7. (2)
4. (3)   8. (3)

Unit 3: Resolving Conflict

▼ Lesson 7

Revisit Your Strategy (p. 92)

Answers will vary.

After You Read (p. 93)

A. 1. (4)   4. (3)
2. (2)   5. (2)
3. (4)   6. (1)

B. The following statements should be checked: 2, 4, and 5.

Think About It

B. Practice (p. 95)

1. Sample answers:
   Solution 1: A barking dog is hard to ignore.
   Solution 2: Taping the dog's mouth shut may harm the dog.
   Solution 3: Talking with the neighbors may lead to a mutually agreeable solution.
   Choose the best one: Solution 3
   Step 5: Talk with the neighbors about how much the dog's barking annoys you. Offer to help find a solution. If that fails, check to see if your community has an appropriate ordinance. If not, try mediation.

2a. Sample answers:
   Step 1. State the problem: Neighbors were bothered by a messy willow tree.
   Step 2. Identify the cause: The weeping willow tree needs trimming, but the owners refuse to have it trimmed.
   Step 3. Think of possible solutions.
   Solution 1: Poison the tree.
   Solution 2: Ignore it.
   Solution 3: Talk with the neighbors about it.

Step 4. Evaluate the possible solutions and choose the best one.
Solution 1: This drastic solution could lead to legal action against you.
Solution 2: Ignoring it means the problem will probably get worse.
Solution 3: If everyone involved discusses the problem, they may find a mutually acceptable solution.
Choose the best one: Solution 3
Step 5. Develop a plan to carry out the solution and follow it: Find out why the neighbors won't trim their tree. Offer to help or to share the costs of hiring a professional tree trimming service.

b. Sample answers:
Step 1. State the problem: Rubin was upset when his nap was interrupted.
Step 2. Identify the cause: neighbors playing basketball near your bedroom window.
Step 3. Think of possible solutions.
Solution 1: Ignore it.
Solution 2: Soak the neighbors with a hose.
Solution 3: Discuss the problem with the neighbors.
Step 4. Evaluate the possible solutions and choose the best one.
Solution 1: It may just keep happening if it is ignored.
Solution 2: This could result in legal action against you.
Solution 3: Discussing the problem calmly can lead to a permanent solution.
Choose the best one: Solution 3
Step 5. Develop a plan to carry out the solution and follow it: Wait until you cool down, think about how you want the problem resolved, then talk with the neighbors about it.

▼ Lesson 8

Revisit Your Strategy (p. 104)

Sample answer:

An upset customer may calm down when an employee takes the complaint seriously, listens carefully, and works with the customer to develop a solution.

After You Read (p. 105)

A. 1. (1) 4. (4)
2. (2) 5. (3)
3. (2) 6. (3)

B. The following descriptions should be checked: reassuring, patient, capable, understanding, respectful, sincere, good at listening, cool under fire.

Think About It

B. Practice (p. 107)

1. Sample answers:

Idea	One way you could apply the idea
Verbally cushion the customer's concerns.	Say, "I can understand how you'd feel that way."
Probe for more information; get clarification.	Say, "Let me see if I've got this straight." Then restate the man's problem.
Take immediate action.	Tell the man you are going to get the store manager right away to help with the situation.
See if compensation is possible.	Offer to send a repair person immediately and to install a free icemaker.

2. Answers will vary. Any statements that relate to the general ideas selected are acceptable.
3. Role-play with your partner for the rest of the group.

▼ Lesson 9

Revisit Your Strategy (p. 112)

Answers will vary depending on your imagination. Discuss your answers with the group.

After You Read (p. 113)

A. 1. (2) 4. (3)
2. (4) 5. (2)
3. (3) 6. (1)

B. The following statements should be checked: 1, 2, 4, and 5.

Think About It

B. Practice (p. 115)

1. Sample answer: I can feel his anger. He's so angry that he says all this in one breath, and throws every conflict he has had with the owner into his tantrum. He seems out of control. When he said, "I'm still mad about it," I thought, "No kidding!"

2a. Any of the following: "I think he's a fascist who wants peasant employees." "he thinks I'm a good example of how democracy can be carried too far."

b. "I raved on this way for twenty minutes." "My monologue was delivered at the top of my lungs," "A call to arms, freedom, unions, uprisings, and the breaking of chains for the working masses."

3. Sample answers: "That tears it." "I unloaded," "had it up to here," "sick and tired of this crap," "the whole hotel stinks," horses are nags, guests are idiots, "wouldn't feed that stuff to pigs," "you get the drift," "at the top of my lungs."

4. Sample answers: sat quietly; with sorrowful eyes; a bloodhound in a suit and tie; survivor of Auschwitz, German Jew, thin, coughed a lot, liked peace and quiet, all the wieners and sauerkraut he wanted; to him, a feast.

5. Sample answer: I was struck by the serious comment on life the author concluded with. It made me stop and think. And the final "good night" made me think of Sigmund Wollman, what he went through in his life, and the respectful thanks that the author is paying him.

6. The following should be checked: run-on sentences, sentence fragments, colorful language, interesting details, humor, and exaggeration.

▼ Writing Skills Mini-Lesson: Subject-Verb Agreement (p. 118)

My company **is** offering three workshops. Each of the workshops **is** about a different kind of conflict. The first workshop is called "The Angry Customer." Everybody **seems** to have had a problem with a customer at one time or another. Most customers are polite, but a few **lose** control. A customer of mine once tried to return a shirt, but several of the buttons **were** missing. He shouted, "I want my money back," and started to push me. Luckily, one of the supervisors **was** nearby and came to my rescue.

Employees are human too, and a few **have** begun shouting back. The workshop is supposed to prevent such incidents. Everyone **needs** a calm way to resolve conflicts with customers. The audience **learns** several ways to handle angry customers. My group **is** really looking forward to this workshop.

▼ Unit 3 Review (p. 119)

1. (3)
2. (1)
3. (2)
4. (4)
5. (1)
6. (4)
7. 1-b, 2-a, 3-c, 4-e, 5-d

Unit 4: Attitudes toward Work

▼ Lesson 10

Revisit Your Strategy (p. 130)

All but the first item should be checked.

After You Read (p. 131)

A. 1. (4)
2. (2)
3. (1)
4. (4)
5. (3)
6. (2)

B. The following statements should be checked: 1, 2, and 4.

Think About It

B. Practice (p. 133)

1. Sample answers:

1950s	Fails to get college scholarship Starts junior college Drops out of junior college Plays semi-pro football
1960s	Meets and marries Anna Starts college at Colorado State U. with aid from Steelers Works to get good grades and excels at college football By his third year qualifies to play pro football Plays football for Steelers and becomes All-Pro Starts first fast-food restaurants

2.

1960s	Opens first All-Pro Chicken
	e
1970s	a
	d
1980s	c
1990s	f
	b

▼ Lesson 11

Revisit Your Strategy (p. 138)

1. b
2. c
3. a

After You Read (p. 139)

A. 1. (2)
2. (3)
3. (4)
4. (4)
5. (2)
6. (1)

B. The following statements should be checked: 2, 4, 5, and 8.

Think About It

B. Practice (p. 141)

Sample answers:

1. The following traits should be checked: a, b, c, e, g, and h

2a. exaggeration, vivid images

  b. exaggeration, vivid images, dire predictions

  c. surprise, exaggeration, vivid images, dire predictions

  d. surprise, exaggeration, vivid images, dire predictions

▼ Lesson 12

Revisit Your Strategy (p. 148)

Answers will vary.

After You Read (p. 149)

A. 1. (3)
  2. (4)
  3. (1)
  4. (2)
  5. (2)
  6. (4)

B. The following descriptions should be checked: 1, 4, and 5.

Think About It

B. Practice (p. 151)

Possible answers:

1. Plan: Stay focused on the small details of the task so you can see a common task from a different perspective.

2. Plan: Approach work as game. Make it more challenging, but not so challenging that you become stressed.

3. Problem: Self-consciousness is an obstacle to flow.

  Plan: Focus attention on what's happening with the task itself rather than on yourself and what people think about you.

▼ Writing Skills Mini-Lesson: More Subject-Verb Agreement (p. 154)

1. Leo's <u>attitude</u> toward his job **has** always been positive.

2. How long **have** <u>Leo and his brother</u> worked at Electric City?

3. <u>Leo</u> plus two of his friends **wants** to take management training.

4. Here **are** <u>the schedule and the material</u> for the next training session.

5. Included in the material **is** a <u>manual</u> for trainees.

6. Leo's <u>plans</u> for the future **include** a position in management.

7. <u>One</u> of Leo's dreams **is** to own his own business.

8. There **are** many <u>people</u> with a similar dream.

▼ Unit 4 Review (p. 156)

1. (4)
2. (4)
3. (2)
4. (3)
5. (3)
6. (2)
7. (4)
8. (1)

Writing Skills

This handbook lists the rules you learned in the Writing Skills Mini-Lessons in this book and other information you may find useful.

Commonly Confused Words

There are many words that sound the same or almost the same as other English words. When you write, you need to know how to spell and use these sound-alike words. Here are a few of the most commonly confused words.

1. *Your* and *you're*

   your—a possessive word meaning "belonging to you"
   Do you like **your** job in the factory?

   you're—a contraction of *you are*
   You're working too hard. = **You are** working too hard.

2. *Its* and *it's*

   its—a possessive word meaning "belonging to it"
   That machine seems to have a mind of **its** own.

   it's—a contraction of *it is*
   It's hard to work the night shift. = **It is** hard to work the night shift.

3. *Whose* and *who's*

   whose—a possessive word meaning "belonging to whom"
   Whose job is it, anyway?

   who's—a contraction of *who is* or *who has*
   Who's going to repair the machine? = **Who is** going to repair the machine?
   Who's found the instructions? = **Who has** found the instructions?

4. *There, their,* and *they're*

   there—a word used to introduce a sentence; a word meaning "in that place."
   There should be glue in the storeroom. Look **there** again.

   their—a possessive word meaning "belonging to them"
   Their jobs pay pretty well.

   they're—a contraction of *they are*
   They're working in the factory. = **They are** working in the factory.

Remember: Use an apostrophe to form a contraction. Do not use an apostrophe to form the possessive of pronouns.

Pronoun Agreement

A pronoun is a word that takes the place of a noun. A pronoun must agree with its **antecedent**—the noun that it stands for—three ways: in case, number, and gender.

Antecedent   **Pronoun**

Anita was confined to a wheelchair, but **she** wanted a job.

Case is determined by how the word is used in a sentence. There are three cases:
- **Nominative** for subjects: *I, you, he, she, it, we, you,* and *they.*
- **Objective** for objects of verbs and prepositions: *me, you, him, her, it, us, you,* and *them.*
- **Possessive** to show ownership: *my, mine, your, yours, his, her, hers, its, our, ours, your, yours, their, theirs.*

Number means singular *(I, you, he, she,* and *it)* or plural *(we, you,* and *they).*

Gender means male or female *(he, him, his* or *she, her, hers).*

Follow these rules about pronouns and their antecedents.

1. **Be sure the pronoun has a clear antecedent.** If it is not clear, rewrite the sentence.

   Unclear: Anita talked with her sister about what she could do.
   (About what who could do, Anita or her sister?)
   Clear: **Anita's** sister gave **her** advice about looking for work.

2. **Be sure the pronoun agrees with its antecedent in case, number, and gender.**

   Wrong: **Her** and her sister made a list of jobs Anita could do.
   Right: **She** and her sister made a list of jobs Anita could do.

   Wrong: Each woman tried **their** best to think of all possibilities.
   Right: Each woman tried **her** best to think of all possibilities.

   Wrong: Anita asked one of her friends if **they** would help too.
   Right: Anita asked one of her friends if **she** (or **he**) would help too.

Subject-Verb Agreement

Verbs must agree with their subjects. If the subject is singular, the verb must be singular too. If the subject is plural, the verb must also be plural. Here are a few guidelines for some troublesome subjects.

1. **These words are always singular.** Words ending in *-one, -thing,* or *-body* are singular. So are *each, every,* and *much.*

   > **Everybody was** at the meeting. **No one was** absent. (not *were*)
   > **Each** of the board members **was** scheduled to speak. (not *were*)

2. **These words are always plural.** *Many, several, some, most, both,* and *few* are always plural.

   > **Many have experienced** conflicts at work. (not *has experienced*)
   > **Most are able** to settle their conflicts peacefully. (not *is able*)
   > Fortunately, **few become** violent. (not *becomes*)

3. **Collective nouns are usually singular.** Collective nouns are nouns that stand for a group or collection of people or things. Some examples are *audience, committee, company, crowd, group,* and *team.*

   > The **company offers** a workshop every month. (not *offer*)

   - When a collective noun stands for a group as a whole, use a singular verb.
     > Our **team is going** to attend Friday. (not *are going*)

   - When the individual members of the group are emphasized, use a plural verb.
     > Our **team are going** to attend separate sessions next time.

More Subject-Verb Agreement

Verbs must agree with their subjects. Watch out for these special problems.

1. **Compound subjects.** Subjects joined by *and* are plural. A singular subject followed by such words as *plus, as well as,* and *along with* needs a singular verb.

   Plural: **Leo and his brother are** both in computer sales.

   Singular: **Leo** as well as his brother **sells** a lot of computers.

2. **Interrupting words.** Sometimes a phrase comes between the subject and the verb. To choose the correct verb form, look at the subject. Ignore the interrupting words.

   Singular: Leo's **attitude** toward his duties **is** very positive.

3. **Inverted structure.** In an inverted sentence, the verb comes before the subject. Identify the subject and make the verb agree with it.

   • Many questions have an inverted structure:

   What **are** Leo's **plans** for the future? **Does** his **supervisor** recognize his talent?

   • Sentences beginning with *Here* or *There* followed by a form of *to be* are inverted:

   There **are** many **opportunities** for advancement. Here **is** a **list** of training courses.

   • Sometimes when there is an introductory phrase, the sentence is inverted:

   Included in the training **are** a **course** on budgeting time **and one** on managing money.

The Writing Process

The Writing Process is a series of stages that can help you create a good piece of writing.
These stages are shown below.

1. **Prewrite, or plan your writing.**
   A. Think about your topic.
   B. List ideas about your topic.

   C. Organize your ideas.
   • Decide which ideas you will use.
   • Decide the order in which you will use them.
   • Use an organizing method that works well for you.

2. **Write a first draft.**
   A. Use your ideas from stage 1. Also add, drop, or change ideas as you see fit.

   B. Write about your topic.
   • Clearly state your main idea.
   • Give specific details—facts, examples, reasons—to support your main idea.
   • Group related ideas in paragraphs.
   • Include an introduction and a conclusion.

3. **Revise your first draft.**
   A. Check that your first draft
   _____ includes your important ideas
   _____ develops your topic with supporting details
   _____ is clear and easy to understand
   _____ uses clue words to signal the organization of your ideas to your reader
   _____ has an introduction and a conclusion

   B. Make changes to improve your writing.
   • Add, cross out, or move ideas.
   • Reword ideas to make them clearer.
   • Combine related ideas in sentences

4. **Edit your work.**
   A. Check your draft for
   _____ complete sentences
   _____ correct spelling
   _____ correct punctuation
   _____ correct capitalization
   _____ correct usage and grammar

   B. Correct any mistakes you find. If you need help, use the Writing Skills Handbook on pages 172–175 or ask your instructor.

5. **Recopy your draft.**
   A. Write a final draft. Include all of your revising and editing changes.
   B. Compare your first and final drafts. Note improvements.

   C. Share your final draft with a classmate, a friend, or your instructor.

Reading and Writing for Today's Adults

Voyager

8

Karen Harrington

Advisers to the Series

Mary Dunn Siedow
Director
North Carolina Literacy Resource Center
Raleigh, NC

Linda Thistlethwaite
Associate Director
The Central Illinois Adult Education Service Center
Western Illinois University
Macomb, IL

Reviewer

Phyllis Klein
St. George School
Auxiliary Service for High Schools
New York, NY

New Readers Press

Acknowledgments

Ballard, Donna. Reprinted from *Doing It for Ourselves: Success Stories of African-American Women in Business.* Copyright 1997 by Donna Ballard. Permission granted by The Berkley Publishing Group. All rights reserved.

Boe, Deborah. "Factory Work" by Deborah Boe. This poem first appeared in *Poetry.* Reprinted by permission of the author.

Campbell, Bebe Moore. Reprinted by permission of The Putnam Publishing Group from *Brothers and Sisters* by Bebe Moore Campbell. Copyright © 1994 by Bebe Moore Campbell.

Charlton, George. Reprinted by permission of Bloodaxe Books Ltd. from "Nightshift Workers" by George Charlton. (Bloodaxe Books, 1988).

Fulghum, Robert. From *Uh-Oh* by Robert Fulghum. Copyright © 1991 by Robert Fulghum. Reprinted by permission of Villard Books, a division of Random House, Inc and HarperCollins Publishers, Ltd.

Gill, Mark Stuart. "The Neighbors from Hell" by Mark Stuart Gill, *Ladies Home Journal,* June 1994. © Copyright 1994, Meredith Corporation. All rights reserved. Used with the permission of **Ladies Home Journal**® magazine.

Golin, Mark, Mark Briklin and David Dummond. Reprinted from *Secrets of Executive Success* by Mark Golin, Mark Briklin and David Dummond. Permission granted by Rodale Press, Inc., Emmaus, PA 18098. For ordering information, please call 1-800-848-4735.

Grier, Roosevelt. "Brady Keys, Jr." from *Rosey Grier's All-American Heroes* by Roosevelt "Rosey" Grier. Copyright © 1993 Roosevelt "Rosey" Grier. Reprinted by permission of Alexander Hoyt Associates.

Griffin, Katherine. "Getting into the Flow" by Katherine Griffin, *Health,* October 1994. Reprinted with permission from *Health,* © 1994.

Grodin, Charles. "Getting Fired" from *How I Get Through Life* by Charles Grodin. Copyright © 1992 by Charles Grodin. Reprinted by permission of William Morrow & Company, Inc. and The Robert Lantz-Joy Harris Literary Agency.

Johnson, David W. From *Reaching Out: Interpersonal Effectiveness and Self-Actualization, 2E* by David W. Johnson. Reprinted by permission of the author.

Leonard, Sam. From *Mediation: The Book* by Sam Leonard, Evanston, IL. Evanston Publishing Inc., 1994. Reprinted by permission.

"Mamon Powers Jr." Copyright August 1995. Reprinted with Permission, BLACK ENTERPRISE Magazine, New York, NY. All rights reserved.

Piercy, Marge. "To be of use" copyright © 1973, 1982 by Marge Piercy and Middlemarsh, Inc. Published in CIRCLES ON THE WATER: Selected Poems of Marge Piercy, Alfred A. Knopf, Inc. 1982. Used by permission of the Wallace Literary Agency, Inc.

Rooney, Andrew A. Reprinted with the permission of Scribner, a Division of Simon & Schuster from PIECES OF MY MIND by Andy Rooney. Copyright © 1984 by Essay Productions, Inc.

Shawn, Wallace. From *Aunt Dan and Lemon* by Wallace Shawn. Copyright © 1985 by Wallace Shawn. Used by permission of Grove/Atlantic, Inc.

Smith-Yackel, Bonnie. "My Mother Never Worked" By Bonnie Smith-Yackel, from *Women: A Journal of Liberation,* Vol. 4, No. 2, Spring 1975. © Women: A Journal of Liberation. Used by permission.

Swerdlow, Marian. "Marian Swerdlow: Subway Conductor" by Marian Swerdlow. © 1988 Marian Swerdlow. Reprinted from *Hard-Hatted Women: Stories of Struggle and Success in the Trades* edited by Molly Martin. (Seal Press, Seattle). Used by permission.

Terkel, Studs. From *The Great Divide* by Studs Terkel. Copyright © 1988 by Studs Terkel. Reprinted by permission of Pantheon Books, a division of Random House, Inc. and Donadio & Ashworth, Inc.

Ulloa, Yolanda. "Short Biography of a Washerwoman" by Yolanda Ulloa from *Breaking the Silences: Twentieth Century Poetry by Cuban Women* edited and translated by Margaret Randall. (Pulp Press, 1982)

Yoshida, Jim, and Bill Hosokawa. "Two Worlds" from *The Two Worlds of Jim Yoshida* by Jim Yoshida and Bill Hosokawa. Reprinted by permission.

Voyager: Reading and Writing for Today's Adults™ Voyager 8
ISBN 1-56420-158-9
Copyright © 1999
New Readers Press
U.S. Publishing Division of Laubach Literacy International
Box 131, Syracuse, New York 13210-0131

Printed in the United States of America
9 8 7 6 5 4 3 2

Director of Acquisitions and Development: Christina Jagger
Content Editor: Mary Hutchison
Developer: Learning Unlimited, Oak Park, IL
Developmental Editor: Pamela Bliss
Contributing Writer: Betsy Rubin
Production Director: Jennifer Lohr
Photography: David Revette Photography, Inc.
Cover Design: Gerald Russell
Designer: Kimbrly Koennecke
Copy Editor: Judi Lauber
Artist/Illustrator: Linda Tiff, Patricia A. Rapple

Contents